ANDROCLES AND THE LION

ANDROCLES
AND THE LION

by

BERNARD SHAW

with an Introduction
and Notes by

A. C. WARD

Longmans, Green and Co
in association with
Constable and Co Ltd

LONGMANS, GREEN AND CO LTD
48 Grosvenor Street, London W.1
*Associated companies, branches and representatives
throughout the world*

*This Edition first published 1957
Second impression 1960
Third impression 1963
Fourth impression 1963*

PRINTED IN GREAT BRITAIN
BY R. & R. CLARK, LTD., EDINBURGH

CONTENTS

PREFACE ON THE PROSPECTS OF CHRISTIANITY

Why not give Christianity a Trial?

THE question seems a hopeless one after 2000 years of resolute adherence to the old cry of "Not this man, but Barabbas." Yet it is beginning to look as if Barabbas was a failure, in spite of his strong right hand, his victories, his empires, his millions of money, and his moralities and churches and political constitutions. "This man" has not been a failure yet; for nobody has ever been sane enough to try his way. But he has had one quaint triumph. Barabbas has stolen his name and taken his cross as a standard. There is a sort of compliment in that. There is even a sort of loyalty in it, like that of the brigand who breaks every law and yet claims to be a patriotic subject of the king who makes them. We have always had a curious feeling that though we crucified Christ on a stick, he somehow managed to get hold of the right end of it, and that if we were better men we might try his plan. There have been one or two grotesque attempts at it by inadequate people, such as the Kingdom of God in Munster, which was ended by a crucifixion so much more atrocious than the one on Calvary that the bishop who took the part of Annas went home and died of horror. But responsible people have never made such attempts. The moneyed, respectable, capable world has been steadily anti-Christian and Barabbasque since the crucifixion; and the specific doctrine of Jesus has not in all that time been put into political or general social practice. I am no more a Christian than Pilate was, or you, gentle reader; and yet, like Pilate, I greatly prefer Jesus to Annas and Caiaphas; and I am ready to admit that after contemplating the world and human nature for nearly sixty years, I see no way out of the world's misery but the way which would have been found by Christ's will if he had undertaken the work of a modern practical statesman.

Pray do not at this early point lose patience with me and shut the book. I assure you I am as sceptical and scientific and modern a thinker as you will find anywhere. I grant you I know a great deal more about economics and politics than Jesus did, and can do things he could not do. I am by all Barabbasque standards a person of much better character and standing, and greater practical sense. I have no sympathy with vagabonds and talkers who try to reform society by taking men away from their regular productive work and making vagabonds and talkers of them too; and if I had been Pilate I should have recognized as plainly as he the necessity for suppressing attacks on the existing social order, however corrupt that order might be, by people with no knowledge of government and no power to construct political machinery to carry out their views, acting on the very dangerous delusion that the end of the world was at hand. I make no defence of such Christians as Savonarola and John of Leyden: they were scuttling the ship before they had learned how to build a raft; and it became necessary to throw them overboard to save the crew. I say this to set myself right with respectable society; but I must still insist that if Jesus could have worked out the practical problems of a Communist constitution, an admitted obligation to deal with crime without revenge or punishment, and a full assumption by humanity of divine responsibilities, he would have conferred an incalculable benefit on mankind, because these distinctive demands of his are now turning out to be good sense and sound economics.

I say distinctive, because his common humanity and his subjection to time and space (that is, to the Syrian life of his period) involved his belief in many things, true and false, that in no way distinguish him from other Syrians of that time. But such common beliefs do not constitute specific Christianity any more than wearing a beard, working in a carpenter's shop, or believing that the earth is flat and that the stars could drop on it from heaven like hailstones. Christianity interests practical statesmen now because of the doctrines that distinguished Christ from the Jews and the Barabbasques generally, including ourselves.

WHY JESUS MORE THAN ANOTHER?

I do not imply, however, that these doctrines were peculiar to Christ. A doctrine peculiar to one man would be only a craze, unless its comprehension depended on a development of human faculty so rare that only one exceptionally gifted man possessed it. But even in this case it would be useless, because incapable of spreading. Christianity is a step in moral evolution which is independent of any individual preacher. If Jesus had never existed (and that he ever existed in any other sense than that in which Shakespear's Hamlet existed has been vigorously questioned) Tolstoy would have thought and taught and quarrelled with the Greek Church all the same. Their creed has been fragmentarily practised to a considerable extent in spite of the fact that the laws of all countries treat it, in effect, as criminal. Many of its advocates have been militant atheists. But for some reason the imagination of white mankind has picked out Jesus of Nazareth as *the* Christ, and attributed all the Christian doctrines to him; and as it is the doctrine and not the man that matters, and, as, besides, one symbol is as good as another provided everyone attaches the same meaning to it, I raise, for the moment, no question as to how far the gospels are original, and how far they consist of Greek and Chinese interpolations. The record that Jesus said certain things is not invalidated by a demonstration that Confucius said them before him. Those who claim a literal divine paternity for him cannot be silenced by the discovery that the same claim was made for Alexander and Augustus. And I am not just now concerned with the credibility of the gospels as records of fact; for I am not acting as a detective, but turning our modern lights on to certain ideas and doctrines in them which disentangle themselves from the rest because they are flatly contrary to common practice, common sense, and common belief, and yet have, in the teeth of dogged incredulity and recalcitrance, produced an irresistible impression that Christ, though rejected by his posterity as an unpractical dreamer, and executed by his contemporaries as a dangerous anarchist and blasphemous madman, was greater than his judges.

WAS JESUS A COWARD?

I know quite well that this impression of superiority is not produced on everyone, even of those who profess extreme susceptibility to it. Setting aside the huge mass of inculcated Christworship which has no real significance because it has no intelligence, there is, among people who are really free to think for themselves on the subject, a great deal of hearty dislike of Jesus and of contempt for his failure to save himself and overcome his enemies by personal bravery and cunning as Mahomet did. I have heard this feeling expressed far more impatiently by persons brought up in England as Christians than by Mahometans, who are, like their prophet, very civil to Jesus, and allow him a place in their esteem and veneration at least as high as we accord to John the Baptist. But this British bulldog contempt is founded on a complete misconception of his reasons for submitting voluntarily to an ordeal of torment and death. The modern Secularist is often so determined to regard Jesus as a man like himself and nothing more, that he slips unconsciously into the error of assuming that Jesus shared that view. But it is quite clear from the New Testament writers (the chief authorities for believing that Jesus ever existed) that Jesus at the time of his death believed himself to be the Christ, a divine personage. It is therefore absurd to criticize his conduct before Pilate as if he were Colonel Roosevelt or Admiral von Tirpitz or even Mahomet. Whether you accept his belief in his divinity as fully as Simon Peter did, or reject it as a delusion which led him to submit to torture and sacrifice his life without resistance in the conviction that he would presently rise again in glory, you are equally bound to admit that, far from behaving like a coward or a sheep, he shewed considerable physical fortitude in going through a cruel ordeal against which he could have defended himself as effectually as he cleared the money-changers out of the temple. "Gentle Jesus, meek and mild" is a snivelling modern invention, with no warrant in the gospels. St Matthew would as soon have thought of applying such adjectives to Judas Maccabeus as to Jesus; and even St Luke, who makes Jesus polite and gracious, does not make him meek. The picture of him as an English curate of the farcical comedy type, too meek to fight a policeman, and everybody's butt, may be useful in the nursery to soften children; but that such a figure could ever have become a centre of the world's attention is too absurd for discussion: grown men and women may speak kindly of a harmless creature who utters amiable sentiments and is a helpless nincompoop when he is called on to defend them; but they will not follow him, nor do what he tells them, because they do not wish to share his defeat and disgrace.

Was Jesus a Martyr?

It is important therefore that we should clear our minds of the notion that Jesus died, as some of us are in the habit of declaring, for his social and political opinions. There have been many martyrs to those opinions; but he was not one of them, nor, as his words shew, did he see any more sense in martyrdom than Galileo did. He was executed by the Jews for the blasphemy of claiming to be a God; and Pilate, to whom this was a mere piece of superstitious nonsense, let them execute him as the cheapest way of keeping them quiet, on the formal plea that he had committed treason against Rome by saying that he was the King of the Jews. He was not falsely accused, nor denied full opportunities of defending himself. The proceedings were quite straightforward and regular; and Pilate, to whom the appeal lay, favored him and despised his judges, and was evidently willing enough to be conciliated. But instead of denying the charge, Jesus repeated the offence. He knew what he was doing: he had alienated numbers of his own disciples and been stoned in the streets for doing it before. He was not lying: he believed literally what he said. The horror of the High Priest was perfectly natural: he was a Primate confronted with a heterodox street preacher uttering what seemed to him an appalling and impudent blasphemy. The fact that the blasphemy was to Jesus a simple statement of fact, and that it has since been accepted as such by all western nations, does not invalidate the proceedings, nor give us the right to regard Annas and Caiaphas as worse men than the Archbishop of Canterbury and the Head Master of Eton. If Jesus had been indicted in a modern court, he would have been examined by two doctors; found to be obsessed by a delusion; declared incapable of pleading; and sent to an asylum: that is the whole difference. But please note that when a man is charged before a modern tribunal (to take a case that happened the other day) of having asserted and maintained that he was an officer returned from the front to receive the Victoria Cross at the hands of the King, although he was in fact a mechanic, nobody thinks of treating him as afflicted with a delusion. He is punished for false pretences, because his assertion is credible and therefore misleading. Just so, the claim to divinity made by Jesus was to the High Priest, who looked forward to the coming of a Messiah, one that might conceivably have been true, and might therefore have misled the people in a very dangerous way. That was why he treated Jesus as an impostor and a blasphemer where we should have treated him as a madman.

THE GOSPELS WITHOUT PREJUDICE

All this will become clear if we read the gospels without prejudice. When I was young it was impossible to read them without fantastic confusion of thought. The confusion was so utterly confounded that it was called the proper spirit to read the Bible in. Jesus was a baby; and he was older than creation. He was a man who could be persecuted, stoned, scourged, and killed; and he was a god, immortal and all-powerful, able to raise the dead and call millions of angels to his aid. It was a sin to doubt either view of him: that is, it was a sin to reason about him; and the end was that you did not reason about him, and read about him only when you were compelled. When you heard the gospel stories read in church, or learnt them from painters and poets, you came out with an impression of their contents that would have astonished a Chinaman who had read the story without prepossession. Even sceptics who were specially on their guard, put the Bible in the dock, and read the gospels with the object of detecting discrepancies in the four narratives to shew that the writers were as subject to error as the writers of yesterday's newspaper.

All this has changed greatly within two generations. Today the Bible is so little read that the language of the Authorized Version is rapidly becoming obsolete; so that even in the United States, where the old tradition of the verbal infallibility of "the book of books" lingers more strongly than anywhere else except perhaps in Ulster, retranslations into modern English have been introduced perforce to save its bare intelligibility. It is quite easy today to find cultivated persons who have never read the New Testament, and on whom therefore it is possible to try the experiment of asking them to read the gospels and state what they have gathered as to the history and views and character of Christ.

THE GOSPELS NOW UNINTELLIGIBLE TO NOVICES

But it will not do to read the gospels with a mind furnished only for the reception of, say, a biography of Goethe. You will not make sense of them, nor even be able without impatient weariness to persevere in the task of going steadily through them, unless you know something of the history of the human imagination as applied to religion. Not long ago I asked a writer of distinguished intellectual competence whether he had made a study of the gospels since his childhood. His reply was that he had lately tried, but "found it all such nonsense that I could not stick it." As I do not want to send anyone to the gospels with this result, I had better here give a brief exposition of how much of the history of religion is needed to make the gospels and the conduct and ultimate fate of Jesus intelligible and interesting.

WORLDLINESS OF THE MAJORITY

The first common mistake to get rid of is that mankind consists of a great mass of religious people and a few eccentric atheists. It consists of a huge mass of worldly people, and a small percentage of persons deeply interested in religion and concerned about their own souls and other people's; and this section consists mostly of those who are passionately affirming the established religion and those who are passionately attacking it, the genuine philosophers being very few. Thus you never have a nation of millions of Wesleys and one Tom Paine. You have a million Mr Worldly Wisemans, one Wesley, with his small congregation, and one Tom Paine, with *his* smaller congregation. The passionately religious are a people apart; and if they were not hopelessly outnumbered by the worldly, they would turn the world upside down, as St Paul was reproached, quite justly, for wanting to do. Few people can number among their personal acquaintances a single atheist or a single Plymouth Brother. Unless a religious turn in ourselves has led us to seek the little Societies to which these rare birds belong, we pass our lives among people who, whatever creeds they may repeat, and in whatever temples they may avouch their respectability and wear their Sunday clothes, have robust consciences, and hunger and thirst, not for righteousness, but for rich feeding and comfort and social position and attractive mates and ease and pleasure and respect and consideration: in short, for love and money. To these people one morality is as good as another provided they are used to it and can put up with its restrictions without unhappiness; and in the maintenance of this morality they will fight and punish and coerce without scruple. They may not be the salt of the earth, these Philistines; but they are the substance of civilization; and they save society from ruin by criminals and conquerors as well as by Savonarolas and Knipperdollings. And as they know, very sensibly, that a little religion is good for children and serves morality, keeping the poor in goodhumor or in awe by promising rewards in heaven or threatening torments in hell, they encourage the religious people up to a certain point: for instance, if Savonarola only tells the ladies of Florence that they ought to tear off their jewels and finery and sacrifice them to God, they offer him a cardinal's hat, and praise him as a saint; but if he induces them to actually do it, they burn him as a public nuisance.

RELIGION OF THE MINORITY. SALVATIONISM

The religion of the tolerated religious minority has always been essentially the same religion: that is why its changes of name and form have made so little difference. That is why, also, a nation so civilized as the English can convert negroes to their faith with great ease, but cannot convert Mahometans or Jews. The negro finds in civilized Salvationism an unspeakably more comforting version of his crude creed; but neither Saracen nor Jew sees any advantage in it over his own version. The Crusader was surprised to find the Saracen quite as religious and moral as himself, and rather more than less civilized. The Latin Christian has nothing to offer the Greek Christian that Greek Christianity has not already provided. They are all, at root, Salvationists.

Let us trace this religion of Salvation from its beginnings. So many things that man does not himself contrive or desire are always happening: death, plagues, tempests, blights, floods, sunrise and sunset, growths and harvests and decay, and Kant's two wonders of the starry heavens above us and the moral law within us, that we conclude that somebody must be doing it all, or that somebody is doing the good and somebody else doing the evil, or that armies of invisible persons, beneficent and malevolent, are doing it; hence you postulate gods and devils, angels and demons. You propitiate these powers with presents, called sacrifices, and flatteries, called praises. Then the Kantian moral law within you makes you conceive your god as a judge; and straightway you try to corrupt him, also with presents and flatteries. This seems shocking to us; but our objection to it is quite a recent development: no longer ago than Shakespear's time it was thought quite natural that litigants should give presents to human judges; and the buying off of divine wrath by actual money payments to priests, or, in the reformed churches which discountenance this, by subscriptions to charities and church building and the like, is still in full swing. Its practical disadvantage is that though it makes matters very easy for the rich, it cuts off the poor from all hope of divine favor. And this quickens the moral criticism of the poor to such an extent, that they soon find the moral law within them revolting against the idea of buying off the deity with gold and gifts, though are still quite ready to buy him off with the paper money of praise and professions of repentance. Accordingly, you will find that though a religion may last unchanged for many centuries in primitive communities where the conditions of life leave no room for poverty and riches, and the process of propitiating the supernatural powers is as well within the means of the least of the members as within those of the headman, yet when commercial civilization arrives, and capitalism divides the people into a few rich and a great many so poor that they can barely live, a movement for religious reform will arise among the poor, and will be essentially a movement for cheap or entirely gratuitous salvation.

To understand what the poor mean by propitiation, we must examine for a moment what they mean by justice.

THE DIFFERENCE BETWEEN ATONEMENT AND PUNISHMENT

The primitive idea of justice is partly legalized revenge and partly expiation by sacrifice. It works out from both sides in the notion that two blacks make a white, and that when a wrong has been done, it should be paid for by an equivalent suffering. It seems to the Philistine majority a matter of course that this compensating suffering should be inflicted on the wrongdoer for the sake of its deterrent effect on other would-be wrongdoers; but a moment's reflection will shew that this utilitarian application corrupts the whole transaction. For example, the shedding of innocent blood cannot be balanced by the shedding of guilty blood. Sacrificing a criminal to propitiate God for the murder of one of his righteous servants is like sacrificing a mangy sheep or an ox with the rinderpest: it calls down divine wrath instead of appeasing it. In doing it we offer God as a sacrifice the gratification of our own revenge and the protection of our own lives without cost to ourselves; and cost to ourselves is the essence of sacrifice and expiation. However much the Philistines have succeeded in confusing these things in practice, they are to the Salvationist sense distinct and even contrary. The Baronet's cousin in Dickens's novel, who, perplexed by the failure of the police to discover the murderer of the baronet's solicitor, said "Far better hang wrong fellow than no fellow," was not only expressing a very common sentiment, but trembling on the brink of the rarer Salvationist opinion that it is much better to hang the wrong fellow: that, in fact, the wrong fellow is the right fellow to hang.

The point is a cardinal one, because until we grasp it not only does historical Christianity remain unintelligible to us, but those who do not care a rap about historical Christianity may be led into the mistake of supposing that if we discard revenge, and treat murderers exactly as God treated Cain: that is, exempt them from punishment by putting a brand on them as unworthy to be sacrificed, and let them face the world as best they can with that brand on them, we should get rid both of punishment and sacrifice. It would not at all follow: on the contrary, the feeling that there must be an expiation of the murder might quite possibly lead to our putting some innocent person—the more innocent the better—to a cruel death to balance the account with divine justice.

B

Salvation at first a Class Privilege; and the Remedy

Thus, even when the poor decide that the method of purchasing salvation by offering rams and goats or bringing gold to the altar must be wrong because they cannot afford it, we still do not feel "saved" without a sacrifice and a victim. In vain do we try to substitute mystical rites that cost nothing, such as circumcision, or, as a substitute for that, baptism. Our sense of justice still demands an expiation, a sacrifice, a sufferer for our sins. And this leaves the poor man still in his old difficulty; for if it was impossible for him to procure rams and goats and shekels, how much more impossible is it for him to find a neighbor who will voluntarily suffer for his sins: one who will say cheerfully "You have committed a murder. Well, never mind: I am willing to be hanged for it in your stead"?

Our imagination must come to our rescue. Why not, instead of driving ourselves to despair by insisting on a separate atonement by a separate redeemer for every sin, have one great atonement and one great redeemer to compound for the sins of the world once for all? Nothing easier, nothing cheaper. The yoke is easy, the burden light. All you have to do when the redeemer is once found (or invented by the imagination) is to believe in the efficacy of the transaction, and you are saved. The rams and goats cease to bleed; the altars which ask for expensive gifts and continually renewed sacrifices are torn down; and the Church of the single redeemer and the single atonement rises on the ruins of the old temples, and becomes a single Church of the Christ.

Retrospective Atonement; and the Expectation of the Redeemer

But this does not happen at once. Between the old costly religion of the rich and the new gratuitous religion of the poor there comes an interregnum in which the redeemer, though conceived by the human imagination, is not yet found. He is awaited and expected under the names of the Christ, the Messiah, Baldur the Beautiful, or what not; but he has not yet come. Yet the sinners are not therefore in despair. It is true that they cannot say, as we say, "The Christ has come, and has redeemed us"; but they can say "The Christ will come, and will redeem us," which, as the atonement is conceived as retrospective, is equally consoling. There are periods when nations are seething with this expectation and crying aloud with prophecy of the Redeemer through their poets. To feel that atmosphere we have only to take up the Bible and read Isaiah at one end of such a period and Luke and John at the other.

COMPLETION OF THE SCHEME BY LUTHER AND CALVIN

We now see our religion as a quaint but quite intelligible evolution from crude attempts to propitiate the destructive forces of Nature among savages to a subtle theology with a costly ritual of sacrifice possible only to the rich as a luxury, and finally to the religion of Luther and Calvin. And it must be said for the earlier forms that they involved very real sacrifices. The sacrifice was not always vicarious, and is not yet universally so. In India men pay with their own skins, torturing themselves hideously to attain holiness. In the west, saints amazed the world with their austerities and self-scourgings and confessions and vigils. But Luther delivered us from all that. His reformation was a triumph of imagination and a triumph of cheapness. It brought you complete salvation and asked you for nothing but faith. Luther did not know what he was doing in the scientific sociological way in which we know it; but his instinct served him better than knowledge could have done; for it was instinct rather than theological casuistry that made him hold so resolutely to Justification by Faith as the trump card by which he should beat the Pope, or, as he would have put it, the sign in which he should conquer. He may be said to have abolished the charge for admission to heaven. Paul had advocated this; but Luther and Calvin did it.

JOHN BARLEYCORN

There is yet another page in the history of religion which must be conned and digested before the career of Jesus can be fully understood. People who can read long books will find it in Frazer's Golden Bough. Simpler folk will find it in the peasant's song of John Barleycorn, now made accessible to our drawing room amateurs in the admirable collections of Somersetshire Folk Songs by Mr Cecil Sharp. From Frazer's *magnum opus* you will learn how the same primitive logic which makes the Englishman believe today that by eating a beefsteak he can acquire the strength and courage of the bull, and to hold that belief in the face of the most ignominious defeats by vegetarian wrestlers and racers and bicyclists, led the first men who conceived God as capable of incarnation to believe that they could acquire a spark of his divinity by eating his flesh and drinking his blood. And from the song of John Barleycorn you may learn how the miracle of the seed, the growth, and the harvest, still the most wonderful of all the miracles and as inexplicable as ever, taught the primitive husband-man, and, as we must now affirm, taught him quite rightly, that God is in the seed, and that God is immortal. And thus it became the test of Godhead that nothing that you could do to it could kill it, and that when you buried it, it would rise again in renewed life and beauty and give mankind eternal life on condition that it was eaten and drunk, and again slain and buried, to rise again for ever and ever. You may, and indeed must, use John Barleycorn "right barbarouslee," cutting him "off at knee" with your scythes, scourging him with your flails, burying him in the earth; and he will not resist you nor reproach you, but will rise again in golden beauty amidst a great burst of sunshine and bird music, and save you and renew your life. And from the interweaving of these two traditions with the craving for the Redeemer, you at last get the conviction that when the Redeemer comes he will be immortal; he will give us his body to eat and his blood to drink; and he will prove his divinity by suffering a barbarous death without resistance or reproach, and rise from the dead and return to the earth in glory as the giver of life eternal.

LOOKING FOR THE END OF THE WORLD

Yet another persistent belief has beset the imagination of the religious ever since religion spread among the poor, or, rather, ever since commercial civilization produced a hopelessly poor class cut off from enjoyment in this world. That belief is that the end of this world is at hand, and that it will presently pass away and be replaced by a kingdom of happiness, justice, and bliss in which the rich and the oppressors and the unjust shall have no share. We are all familiar with this expectation: many of us cherish some pious relative who sees in every great calamity a sign of the approaching end. Warning pamphlets are in constant circulation: advertisements are put in the papers and paid for by those who are convinced, and who are horrified at the indifference of the irreligious to the approaching doom. And revivalist preachers, now as in the days of John the Baptist, seldom fail to warn their flocks to watch and pray, as the great day will steal upon them like a thief in the night, and cannot be long deferred in a world so wicked. This belief also associates itself with Barleycorn's second coming; so that the two events become identified at last.

There is the other and more artificial side of this belief, on which it is an inculcated dread. The ruler who appeals to the prospect of heaven to console the poor and keep them from insurrection also curbs the vicious by threatening them with hell. In the Koran we find Mahomet driven more and more to this expedient of government; and experience confirms his evident belief that it is impossible to govern without it in certain phases of civilization. We shall see later on that it gives a powerful attraction to the belief in a Redeemer, since it adds to remorse of conscience, which hardened men bear very lightly, a definite dread of hideous and eternal torture.

The Honor of Divine Parentage

One more tradition must be noted. The consummation of praise for a king is to declare that he is the son of no earthly father, but of a god. His mother goes into the temple of Apollo, and Apollo comes to her in the shape of a serpent, or the like. The Roman emperors, following the example of Augustus, claimed the title of God. Illogically, such divine kings insist a good deal on their royal human ancestors. Alexander, claiming to be the son of Apollo, is equally determined to be the son of Philip. As the gospels stand, St Matthew and St Luke give genealogies (the two are different) establishing the descent of Jesus through Joseph from the royal house of David, and yet declare that not Joseph but the Holy Ghost was the father of Jesus. It is therefore now held that the story of the Holy Ghost is a later interpolation borrowed from the Greek and Roman imperial tradition. But experience shews that simultaneous faith in the descent from David and the conception by the Holy Ghost is possible. Such double beliefs are entertained by the human mind without uneasiness or consciousness of the contradiction involved. Many instances might be given: a familiar one to my generation being that of the Tichborne claimant, whose attempt to pass himself off as a baronet was supported by an association of laborers on the ground that the Tichborne family, in resisting it, were trying to do a laborer out of his rights. It is quite possible that Matthew and Luke may have been unconscious of the contradiction: indeed the interpolation theory does not remove the difficulty, as the interpolators themselves must have been unconscious of it. A better ground for suspecting interpolation is that St Paul knew nothing of the divine birth, and taught that Jesus came into the world at his birth as the son of Joseph, but rose from the dead after three days as the son of God. Here again, few notice the discrepancy: the three views are accepted simultaneously without intellectual discomfort. We can provisionally entertain half a dozen contradictory versions of an event if we feel either that it does not greatly matter, or that there is a category attainable in which the contradictions are reconciled.

But that is not the present point. All that need be noted here is that the legend of divine birth was sure to be attached sooner or later to very eminent persons in Roman imperial times, and that modern theologians, far from discrediting it, have very logically affirmed the miraculous conception not only of Jesus but of his mother.

With no more scholarly equipment than a knowledge of these habits of the human imagination, anyone may now read the four gospels without bewilderment, and without the contemptuous incredulity which spoils the temper of many modern atheists, or the senseless credulity which sometimes makes pious people force us to shove them aside in emergencies as impracticable lunatics when they ask us to meet violence and injustice with dumb submission in the belief that the strange demeanor of Jesus before Pilate was meant as an example of normal human conduct. Let us admit that without the proper clues the gospels are, to a modern educated person, nonsensical and incredible, whilst the apostles are unreadable. But with the clues, they are fairly plain sailing. Jesus becomes an intelligible and consistent person. His reasons for going "like a lamb to the slaughter" instead of saving himself as Mahomet did, become quite clear. The narrative becomes as credible as any other historical narrative of its period.

MATTHEW

THE ANNUNCIATION: THE MASSACRE: THE FLIGHT

Let us begin with the gospel of Matthew, bearing in mind that it does not profess to be the evidence of an eyewitness. It is a chronicle, founded, like other chronicles, on such evidence and records as the chronicler could get hold of. The only one of the evangelists who professes to give first-hand evidence as an eyewitness naturally takes care to say so; and the fact that Matthew makes no such pretension, and writes throughout as a chronicler, makes it clear that he is telling the story of Jesus as Holinshed told the story of Macbeth, except that, for a reason to be given later on, he must have collected his material and completed his book within the lifetime of persons contemporary with Jesus. Allowance must also be made for the fact that the gospel is written in the Greek language, whilst the first-hand traditions and the actual utterances of Jesus must have been in Aramaic, the dialect of Palestine. These distinctions are important, as you will find if you read Holinshed or Froissart and then read Benvenuto Cellini. You do not blame Holinshed or Froissart for believing and repeating the things they had read or been told, though you cannot always believe these things yourself. But when Cellini tells you that he saw this or did that, and you find it impossible to believe him, you lose patience with him, and are disposed to doubt everything in his autobiography. Do not forget, then, that Matthew is Holinshed and not Benvenuto. The very first pages of his narrative will put your attitude to the test.

Matthew tells us that the mother of Jesus was betrothed to a man of royal pedigree named Joseph, who was rich enough to live in a house in Bethlehem to which kings could bring gifts of gold without provoking any comment. An angel announces to Joseph that Jesus is the son of the Holy Ghost, and that he must not accuse her of infidelity because of her bearing a son of which he is not the father; but this episode disappears from the subsequent narrative: there is no record of its having been told to Jesus, nor any indication of his having any knowledge of it. The narrative, in fact, proceeds in all respects as if the annunciation formed no part of it.

Herod the Tetrarch, believing that a child has been born who will destroy him, orders all the male children to be slaughtered; and Jesus escapes by the flight of his parents into Egypt, whence they return to Nazareth when the danger is over. Here it is necessary to anticipate a little by saying that none of the other evangelists accepts this story, as none of them except John, who throws over Matthew altogether, shares his craze for treating history and biography as mere records of the fulfilment of ancient Jewish prophecies. This craze no doubt led him to seek for some legend bearing out Hosea's "Out of Egypt have I called my son," and Jeremiah's Rachel weeping for her children: in fact, he says so. Nothing that interests us nowadays turns on the credibility of the massacre of the innocents and the flight into Egypt. We may forget them, and proceed to the important part of the narrative, which skips at once to the manhood of Jesus.

JOHN THE BAPTIST

At this moment, a Salvationist prophet named John is stirring the people very strongly. John has declared that the rite of circumcision is insufficient as a dedication of the individual to God, and has substituted the rite of baptism. To us, who are accustomed to baptism as a matter of course, and to whom circumcision is a rather ridiculous foreign practice of no consequence, the sensational effect of such a heresy as this on the Jews is not apparent: it seems to us as natural that John should have baptized people as that the rector of our village should do so. But, as St Paul found to his cost later on, the discarding of circumcision for baptism was to the Jews as startling a heresy as the discarding of transubstantiation in the Mass was to the Catholics of the XVI century.

JESUS JOINS THE BAPTISTS

Jesus entered as a man of thirty (Luke says) into the religious life of his time by going to John the Baptist and demanding baptism from him, much as certain well-to-do young gentlemen forty years ago "joined the Socialists." As far as established Jewry was concerned, he burnt his boats by this action, and cut himself off from the routine of wealth, respectability, and orthodoxy. He then began preaching John's gospel, which, apart from the heresy of baptism, the value of which lay in its bringing the Gentiles (that is, the uncircumcized) within the pale of salvation, was a call to the people to repent of their sins, as the kingdom of heaven was at hand. Luke adds that he also preached the communism of charity; told the surveyors of taxes not to over-assess the taxpayers; and advised soldiers to be content with their wages and not to be violent or lay false accusations. There is no record of John going beyond this.

THE SAVAGE JOHN AND THE CIVILIZED JESUS

Jesus went beyond it very rapidly, according to Matthew. Though, like John, he became an itinerant preacher, he departed widely from John's manner of life. John went into the wilderness, not into the synagogues; and his baptismal font was the river Jordan. He was an ascetic, clothed in skins and living on locusts and wild honey, practising a savage austerity. He courted martyrdom, and met it at the hands of Herod. Jesus saw no merit either in asceticism or martyrdom. In contrast to John he was essentially a highly-civilized, cultivated person. According to Luke, he pointed out the contrast himself, chaffing the Jews for complaining that John must be possessed by the devil because he was a teetotaller and vegetarian, whilst, because Jesus was neither one nor the other, they reviled him as a gluttonous man and a winebibber, the friend of the officials and their mistresses. He told straitlaced disciples that they would have trouble enough from other people without making any for themselves, and that they should avoid martyrdom and enjoy themselves whilst they had the chance. "When they persecute you in this city," he says, "flee into the next." He preaches in the synagogues and in the open air indifferently, just as they come. He repeatedly says, "I desire mercy and not sacrifice," meaning evidently to clear himself of the inveterate superstition that suffering is gratifying to God. "Be not, as the Pharisees, of a sad countenance," he says. He is convivial, feasting with Roman officials and sinners. He is careless of his person, and is remonstrated with for not washing his hands before sitting down to table. The followers of John the Baptist, who fast, and who expect to find the Christians greater ascetics than themselves, are disappointed at finding that Jesus and his twelve friends do not fast; and Jesus tells them that they should rejoice in him instead of being melancholy. He is jocular, and tells them they will all have as much fasting as they want soon enough, whether they like it or not. He is not afraid of disease, and dines with a leper. A woman, apparently to protect him against infection, pours a costly unguent on his head, and is rebuked because what it cost might have been given to the poor. He poohpoohs that lowspirited view, and says, as he said when he was reproached for not fasting, that the poor are always there to be helped, but that he is not there to be anointed always, implying that you should never lose a chance of being happy when there is so much misery in the world. He breaks the Sabbath; is impatient of conventionality when it is uncomfortable or obstructive; and outrages the feelings of the Jews by breaches of it. He is apt to accuse people who feel that way of hypocrisy. Like the late Samuel Butler, he regards disease as a department of sin, and on curing a lame man, says "Thy sins are forgiven" instead of "Arise and walk," subsequently maintaining, when the Scribes reproach him for assuming power to forgive sin as well as to cure disease, that the two come to the same thing. He has no modest affectations, and claims to be greater than Solomon or Jonah. When reproached, as Bunyan was, for resorting to the art of fiction when teaching in parables, he justifies himself on the ground that art is the only way in which the people can be taught. He is, in short, what we should call an artist and a Bohemian in his manner of life.

JESUS NOT A PROSELYTIST

A point of considerable practical importance today is that he expressly repudiates the idea that forms of religion, once rooted, can be weeded out and replanted with the flowers of a foreign faith. "If you try to root up the tares you will root up the wheat as well." Our proselytizing missionary enterprises are thus flatly contrary to his advice; and their results appear to bear him out in his view that if you convert a man brought up in another creed, you inevitably demoralize him. He acts on this view himself, and does not convert his disciples from Judaism to Christianity. To this day a Christian would be in religion a Jew initiated by baptism instead of circumcision, and accepting Jesus as the Messiah, and his teachings as of higher authority than those of Moses, but for the action of the Jewish priests, who, to save Jewry from being submerged in the rising flood of Christianity after the capture of Jerusalem and the destruction of the Temple, set up what was practically a new religious order, with new Scriptures and elaborate new observances, and to their list of the accursed added one Jeschu, a bastard magician, whose comic rogueries brought him to a bad end like Punch or Til Eulenspiegel: an invention which cost them dear when the Christians got the upper hand of them politically. The Jew as Jesus, himself a Jew, knew him, never dreamt of such things, and could follow Jesus without ceasing to be a Jew.

The Teachings of Jesus

So much for his personal life and temperament. His public career as a popular preacher carries him equally far beyond John the Baptist. He lays no stress on baptism or vows, and preaches conduct incessantly. He advocates communism, the widening of the private family with its cramping ties into the great family of mankind under the fatherhood of God, the abandonment of revenge and punishment, the counteracting of evil by good instead of by a hostile evil, and an organic conception of society in which you are not an independent individual but a member of society, your neighbor being another member, and each of you members one of another, as two fingers on a hand, the obvious conclusion being that unless you love your neighbor as yourself and he reciprocates you will both be the worse for it. He conveys all this with extraordinary charm, and entertains his hearers with fables (parables) to illustrate them. He has no synagogue or regular congregation, but travels from place to place with twelve men whom he has called from their work as he passed, and who have abandoned it to follow him.

THE MIRACLES

He has certain abnormal powers by which he can perform miracles. He is ashamed of these powers, but, being extremely compassionate, cannot refuse to exercise them when afflicted people beg him to cure them, when multitudes of people are hungry, and when his disciples are terrified by storms on the lakes. He asks for no reward, but begs the people not to mention these powers of his. There are two obvious reasons for his dislike of being known as a worker of miracles. One is the natural objection of all men who possess such powers, but have far more important business in the world than to exhibit them, to be regarded primarily as charlatans, besides being pestered to give exhibitions to satisfy curiosity. The other is that his view of the effect of miracles upon his mission is exactly that taken later on by Rousseau. He perceives that they will discredit him and divert attention from his doctrine by raising an entirely irrelevant issue between his disciples and his opponents.

Possibly my readers may not have studied Rousseau's Letters Written From The Mountain, which may be regarded as the classic work on miracles as credentials of divine mission. Rousseau shews, as Jesus foresaw, that the miracles are the main obstacle to the acceptance of Christianity, because their incredibility (if they were not incredible they would not be miracles) makes people sceptical as to the whole narrative, credible enough in the main, in which they occur, and suspicious of the doctrine with which they are thus associated. "Get rid of the miracles," said Rousseau, "and the whole world will fall at the feet of Jesus Christ." He points out that miracles offered as evidence of divinity, and failing to convince, make divinity ridiculous. He says, in effect, there is nothing in making a lame man walk: thousands of lame men have been cured and have walked without any miracle. Bring me a man with only one leg and make another grow instantaneously on him before my eyes, and I will be really impressed; but mere cures of ailments that have often been cured before are quite useless as evidence of anything else than desire to help and power to cure.

Jesus, according to Matthew, agreed so entirely with Rousseau, and felt the danger so strongly, that when people who were not ill or in trouble came to him and asked him to exercise his powers as a sign of his mission, he was irritated beyond measure, and refused with an indignation which they, not seeing Rousseau's point, must have thought very unreasonable. To be called "an evil and adulterous generation" merely for asking a miracle worker to give an exhibition of his powers, is rather a startling experience. Mahomet, by the way, also lost his temper when people asked him to perform miracles. But Mahomet expressly disclaimed any unusual powers; whereas it is clear from Matthew's story that Jesus (unfortunately for himself, as he thought) had some powers of healing. It is also obvious that the exercise of such powers would give rise to wild tales of magical feats which would expose their hero to condemnation as an impostor among people whose good opinion was of great consequence to the movement started by his mission.

But the deepest annoyance arising from the miracles would be the irrelevance of the issue raised by them. Jesus's teaching has nothing to do with miracles. If his mission had been simply to demonstrate a new method of restoring lost eyesight, the miracle of curing the blind would have been entirely relevant. But to say "You should love your enemies; and to convince you of this I will now proceed to cure this gentleman of cataract" would have been, to a man of Jesus's intelligence, the proposition of an idiot. If it could be proved today that not one of the miracles of Jesus actually occurred, that proof would not invalidate a single one of his didactic utterances; and conversely, if it could be proved that not only did the miracles actually occur, but that he had wrought a thousand other miracles a thousand times more wonderful, not a jot of weight would be added to his doctrine. And yet the intellectual energy of sceptics and divines has been wasted for generations in arguing about the miracles on the assumption that Christianity is at stake in the controversy as to whether the stories of Matthew are false or true. According to Matthew himself, Jesus must have known this only too well; for wherever he went he was assailed with a clamor for miracles, though his doctrine created bewilderment.

So much for the miracles! Matthew tells us further, that Jesus declared that his doctrines would be attacked by Church and State, and that the common multitude were the salt of the earth and the light of the world. His disciples, in their relations with the political and ecclesiastical organizations, would be as sheep among wolves.

Matthew imputes Bigotry to Jesus

Matthew, like most biographers, strives to identify the opinions and prejudices of his hero with his own. Although he describes Jesus as tolerant even to carelessness, he draws the line at the Gentile, and represents Jesus as a bigoted Jew who regards his mission as addressed exclusively to "the lost sheep of the house of Israel." When a woman of Canaan begged Jesus to cure her daughter, he first refused to speak to her, and then told her brutally that "It is not meet to take the children's bread and cast it to the dogs." But when the woman said, "Truth, Lord; yet the dogs eat of the crumbs which fall from their master's table," she melted the Jew out of him and made Christ a Christian. To the woman whom he had just called a dog he said, "O woman, great is thy faith: be it unto thee even as thou wilt." This is somehow one of the most touching stories in the gospel; perhaps because the woman rebukes the prophet by a touch of his own finest quality. It is certainly out of character; but as the sins of good men are always out of character, it is not safe to reject the story as invented in the interest of Matthew's determination that Jesus shall have nothing to do with the Gentiles. At all events, there the story is; and it is by no means the only instance in which Matthew reports Jesus, in spite of the charm of his preaching, as extremely uncivil in private intercourse.

THE GREAT CHANGE

So far the history is that of a man sane and interesting apart from his special gifts as orator, healer, and prophet. But a startling change occurs. One day, after the disciples have discouraged him for a long time by their misunderstandings of his mission, and their speculations as to whether he is one of the old prophets come again, and if so, which, his disciple Peter suddenly solves the problem by exclaiming, "Thou art the Christ, the son of the living God." At this Jesus is extraordinarily pleased and excited. He declares that Peter has had a revelation straight from God. He makes a pun on Peter's name, and declares him the founder of his Church. And he accepts his destiny as a god by announcing that he will be killed when he goes to Jerusalem; for if he is really the Christ, it is a necessary part of his legendary destiny that he shall be slain. Peter, not understanding this, rebukes him for what seems mere craven melancholy; and Jesus turns fiercely on him and cries, "Get thee behind me, Satan."

Jesus now becomes obsessed with a conviction of his divinity, and talks about it continually to his disciples, though he forbids them to mention it to others. They begin to dispute among themselves as to the position they shall occupy in heaven when his kingdom is established. He rebukes them strenuously for this, and repeats his teaching that greatness means service and not domination; but he himself, always instinctively somewhat haughty, now becomes arrogant, dictatorial, and even abusive, never replying to his critics without an insulting epithet, and even cursing a fig-tree which disappoints him when he goes to it for fruit. He assumes all the traditions of the folk-lore gods, and announces that, like John Barleycorn, he will be barbarously slain and buried, but will rise from the earth and return to life. He attaches to himself the immemorial tribal ceremony of eating the god, by blessing bread and wine and handing them to his disciples with the words "This is my body: this is my blood." He forgets his own teaching and threatens eternal fire and eternal punishment. He announces, in addition to his Barleycorn resurrection, that he will come to the world a second time in glory and establish his kingdom on earth. He fears that this may lead to the appearance of impostors claiming to be himself, and declares explicitly and repeatedly that no matter what wonders these impostors may perform, his own coming will be unmistakeable, as the stars will fall from heaven, and trumpets be blown by angels. Further he declares that this will take place during the lifetime of persons then present.

JERUSALEM AND THE MYSTICAL SACRIFICE

In this new frame of mind he at last enters Jerusalem amid great popular curiosity; drives the moneychangers and sacrifice sellers out of the temple in a riot; refuses to interest himself in the beauties and wonders of the temple building on the ground that presently not a stone of it shall be left on another; reviles the high priests and elders in intolerable terms; and is arrested by night in a garden to avoid a popular disturbance. He makes no resistance, being persuaded that it is part of his destiny as a god to be murdered and to rise again. One of his followers shews fight, and cuts off the ear of one of his captors. Jesus rebukes him, but does not attempt to heal the wound, though he declares that if he wished to resist he could easily summon twelve million angels to his aid. He is taken before the high priest and by him handed over to the Roman governor, who is puzzled by his silent refusal to defend himself in any way, or to contradict his accusers or their wit-

C

nesses, Pilate having naturally no idea that the prisoner conceives himself as going through an inevitable process of torment, death, and burial as a prelude to resurrection. Before the high priest he has also been silent except that when the priest asks him is he the Christ, the Son of God, he replies that they shall all see the Son of Man sitting at the right hand of power, and coming on the clouds of heaven. He maintains this attitude with frightful fortitude whilst they scourge him, mock him, torment him, and finally crucify him between two thieves. His prolonged agony of thirst and pain on the cross at last breaks his spirit, and he dies with a cry of "My God: why hast Thou forsaken me?"

NOT THIS MAN BUT BARABBAS

Meanwhile he has been definitely rejected by the people as well as by the priests. Pilate, pitying him, and unable to make out exactly what he has done (the blasphemy that has horrified the high priest does not move the Roman), tries to get him off by reminding the people that they have, by custom, the right to have a prisoner released at that time, and suggests that he should release Jesus. But they insist on his releasing a prisoner named Barabbas instead, and on having Jesus crucified. Matthew gives no clue to the popularity of Barabbas, describing him simply as "a notable prisoner." The later gospels make it clear, very significantly, that his offence was sedition and insurrection; that he was an advocate of physical force; and that he had killed his man. The choice of Barabbas thus appears as a popular choice of the militant advocate of physical force as against the unresisting advocate of mercy.

THE RESURRECTION

Matthew then tells how after three days an angel opened the family vault of one Joseph, a rich man of Arimathea, who had buried Jesus in it, whereupon Jesus rose and returned from Jerusalem to Galilee and resumed his preaching with his disciples, assuring them that he would now be with them to the end of the world.

At that point the narrative abruptly stops. The story has no ending.

DATE OF MATTHEW'S NARRATIVE

One effect of the promise of Jesus to come again in glory during the lifetime of some of his hearers is to date the gospel without the aid of any scholarship. It must have been written during the lifetime of Jesus's contemporaries: that is, whilst it was still possible for the promise of his Second Coming to be fulfilled. The death of the last person who had been alive when Jesus said "There be some of them that stand here that shall in no wise taste death til they see the Son of Man coming in his kingdom" destroyed the last possibility of the promised Second Coming, and bore out the incredulity of Pilate and the Jews. And as Matthew writes as one believing in that Second Coming, and in fact left his story unfinished to be ended by it, he must have produced his gospel within a lifetime of the crucifixion. Also, he must have believed that reading books would be one of the pleasures of the kingdom of heaven on earth.

CLASS TYPE OF MATTHEW'S JESUS

One more circumstance must be noted as gathered from Matthew. Though he begins his story in such a way as to suggest that Jesus belonged to the privileged classes, he mentions later on that when Jesus attempted to preach in his own country, and had no success there, the people said, "Is not this the carpenter's son?" But Jesus's manner throughout is that of an aristocrat, or at the very least the son of a rich bourgeois, and by no means a lowly-minded one at that. We must be careful therefore to conceive Joseph, not as a modern proletarian carpenter working for weekly wages, but as a master craftsman of royal descent. John the Baptist may have been a Keir Hardie; but the Jesus of Matthew is of the Ruskin-Morris class.

This haughty characterization is so marked that if we had no other documents concerning Jesus than the gospel of Matthew, we should not feel as we do about him. We should have been much less loth to say, "There is a man here who was sane until Peter hailed him as the Christ, and who then became a monomaniac." We should have pointed out that his delusion is a very common delusion among the insane, and that such insanity is quite consistent with the retention of the argumentative cunning and penetration which Jesus displayed in Jerusalem after his delusion had taken complete hold of him. We should feel horrified at the scourging and mocking and crucifixion just as we should if Ruskin had been treated in that way when he also went mad, instead of being cared for as an invalid. And we should have had no clear perception of any special significance in his way of calling the Son of God the Son of Man. We should have noticed that he was a Communist; that he regarded much of what we call law and order as machinery for robbing the poor under legal forms; that he thought domestic ties a snare for the soul; that he agreed with the proverb "The nearer the Church, the farther from God"; that he saw very plainly that the masters of the community should be its servants and not its oppressors and parasites; and that though he did not tell us not to fight our enemies, he did tell us to love them, and warned us that they who draw the sword shall perish by the sword. All this shews a great power of seeing through vulgar illusions, and a capacity for a higher morality than has yet been established in any civilized community; but it does not place Jesus above Confucius or Plato, not to mention more modern philosophers and moralists.

MARK

THE WOMEN DISCIPLES AND THE ASCENSION

Let us see whether we can get anything more out of Mark, whose gospel, by the way, is supposed to be older than Matthew's. Mark is brief; and it does not take long to discover that he adds nothing to Matthew except the ending of the story by Christ's ascension into heaven, and the news that many women had come with Jesus to Jerusalem, including Mary Magdalene, out of whom he had cast seven devils. On the other hand Mark says nothing about the birth of Jesus, and does not touch his career until his adult baptism by John. He apparently regards Jesus as a native of Nazareth, as John does, and not of Bethlehem, as Matthew and Luke do, Bethlehem being the city of David, from whom Jesus is said by Matthew and Luke to be descended. He describes John's doctrine as "Baptism of repentance unto remission of sins": that is, a form of Salvationism. He tells us that Jesus went into the synagogues and taught, not as the Scribes but as one having authority: that is, we infer, he preaches his own doctrine as an original moralist instead of repeating what the books say. He describes the miracle of Jesus reaching the boat by walking across the sea, but says nothing about Peter trying to do the same. Mark sees what he relates more vividly than Matthew, and gives touches of detail that bring the event more clearly before the reader. He says, for instance, that when Jesus walked on the waves to the boat, he was passing it by when the disciples called out to him. He seems to feel that Jesus's treatment of the woman of Canaan requires some apology, and therefore says that she was a Greek of Syrophenician race, which probably excused any incivility to her in Mark's eyes. He represents the father of the boy whom Jesus cured of epilepsy after the transfiguration as a sceptic who says "Lord, I believe: help thou mine unbelief." He tells the story of the widow's mite, omitted by Matthew. He explains that Barabbas was "lying bound with them that made in-

surrection, men who in the insurrection had committed murder."
Joseph of Arimathea, who buried Jesus in his own tomb, and
who is described by Matthew as a disciple, is described by Mark
as "one who also himself was looking for the kingdom of God,"
which suggests that he was an independent seeker. Mark earns
our gratitude by making no mention of the old prophecies, and
thereby not only saves time, but avoids the absurd implication
that Christ was merely going through a predetermined ritual, like
the works of a clock, instead of living. Finally Mark reports
Christ as saying, after his resurrection, that those who believe in
him will be saved and those who do not, damned; but it is impossible to discover whether he means anything by a state of
damnation beyond a state of error. The paleographers regard this
passage as tacked on by a later scribe.

On the whole Mark leaves the modern reader where Matthew
left him.

LUKE

LUKE THE LITERARY ARTIST

When we come to Luke, we come to a later story-teller, and
one with a stronger natural gift for his art. Before you have read
twenty lines of Luke's gospel you are aware that you have passed
from the chronicler writing for the sake of recording important
facts, to the artist, telling the story for the sake of telling it. At the
very outset he achieves the most charming idyll in the Bible: the
story of Mary crowded out of the inn into the stable and laying
her newly-born son in the manger, and of the shepherds abiding
in the field keeping watch over their flocks by night, and how the
angel of the Lord came upon them, and the glory of the Lord
shone around them, and suddenly there was with the angel a
multitude of the heavenly host. These shepherds go to the stable
and take the place of the kings in Matthew's chronicle. So completely has this story conquered and fascinated our imagination

that most of us suppose all the gospels to contain it; but it is Luke's story and his alone: none of the others have the smallest hint of it.

The Charm of Luke's Narrative

Luke gives the charm of sentimental romance to every incident. The Annunciation, as described by Matthew, is made to Joseph, and is simply a warning to him not to divorce his wife for misconduct. In Luke's gospel it is made to Mary herself, at much greater length, with a sense of the ecstasy of the bride of the Holy Ghost. Jesus is refined and softened almost out of recognition: the stern peremptory disciple of John the Baptist, who never addresses a Pharisee or a Scribe without an insulting epithet, becomes a considerate, gentle, sociable, almost urbane person; and the Chauvinist Jew becomes a pro-Gentile who is thrown out of the synagogue in his own town for reminding the congregation that the prophets had sometimes preferred Gentiles to Jews. In fact they try to throw him down from a sort of Tarpeian rock which they use for executions; but he makes his way through them and escapes: the only suggestion of a feat of arms on his part in the gospels. There is not a word of the Syrophenician woman. At the end he is calmly superior to his sufferings; delivers an address on his way to execution with unruffled composure; does not despair on the cross; and dies with perfect dignity, commending his spirit to God, after praying for the forgiveness of his persecutors on the ground that "They know not what they do." According to Matthew, it is part of the bitterness of his death that even the thieves who are crucified with him revile him. According to Luke, only one of them does this; and he is rebuked by the other, who begs Jesus to remember him when he comes into his kingdom. To which Jesus replies, "This day shalt thou be with me in Paradise," implying that he will spend the three days of his death there. In short, every device is used to get rid of the ruthless horror of the Matthew chronicle, and to relieve the strain of the Passion by touching episodes, and by

representing Christ as superior to human suffering. It is Luke's
Jesus who has won our hearts.

THE TOUCH OF PARISIAN ROMANCE

Luke's romantic shrinking from unpleasantness, and his sentimentality, are illustrated by his version of the woman with the
ointment. Matthew and Mark describe it as taking place in the
house of Simon the Leper, where it is objected to as a waste of
money. In Luke's version the leper becomes a rich Pharisee; the
woman becomes a Dame aux Camellias; and nothing is said about
money and the poor. The woman washes the feet of Jesus with
her tears and dries them with her hair; and he is reproached for
suffering a sinful woman to touch him. It is almost an adaptation
of the unromantic Matthew to the Parisian stage. There is a distinct attempt to increase the feminine interest all through. The
slight lead given by Mark is taken up and developed. More is said
about Jesus's mother and her feelings. Christ's following of
women, just mentioned by Mark to account for their presence at
his tomb, is introduced earlier; and some of the women are
named; so that we are introduced to Joanna the wife of Chuza,
Herod's steward, and Susanna. There is the quaint little domestic
episode between Mary and Martha. There is the parable of the
Prodigal Son, appealing to the indulgence romance has always
shewn to Charles Surface and Des Grieux. Women follow Jesus
to the cross; and he makes them a speech beginning "Daughters
of Jerusalem." Slight as these changes may seem, they make a
great change in the atmosphere. The Christ of Matthew could
never have become what is vulgarly called a woman's hero
(though the truth is that the popular demand for sentiment, as
far as it is not simply human, is more manly than womanly); but
the Christ of Luke has made possible those pictures which now
hang in many ladies' chambers, in which Jesus is represented
exactly as he is represented in the Lourdes cinematograph, by a
handsome actor. The only touch of realism which Luke does not

instinctively suppress for the sake of producing this kind of amenity is the reproach addressed to Jesus for sitting down to table without washing his hands; and that is retained because an interesting discourse hangs on it.

Waiting for the Messiah

Another new feature in Luke's story is that it begins in a world in which everyone is expecting the advent of the Christ. In Matthew and Mark, Jesus comes into a normal Philistine world like our own of today. Not until the Baptist foretells that one greater than himself shall come after him does the old Jewish hope of a Messiah begin to stir again; and as Jesus begins as a disciple of John, and is baptized by him, nobody connects him with that hope until Peter has the sudden inspiration which produces so startling an effect on Jesus. But in Luke's gospel men's minds, and especially women's minds, are full of eager expectation of a Christ not only before the birth of Jesus, but before the birth of John the Baptist, the event with which Luke begins his story. Whilst Jesus and John are still in their mothers' wombs, John leaps at the approach of Jesus when the two mothers visit one another. At the circumcision of Jesus pious men and women hail the infant as the Christ.

The Baptist himself is not convinced; for at quite a late period in his former disciple's career he sends two young men to ask Jesus is he really the Christ. This is noteworthy because Jesus immediately gives them a deliberate exhibition of miracles, and bids them tell John what they have seen, and ask him what he thinks *now*. This is in complete contradiction to what I have called the Rousseau view of miracles as inferred from Matthew. Luke shews all a romancer's thoughtlessness about miracles: he regards them as "signs": that is, as proofs of the divinity of the person performing them, and not merely of thaumaturgic powers. He revels in miracles just as he revels in parables: they make such capital stories. He cannot allow the calling of Peter, James, and

John from their boats to pass without a comic miraculous over-draft of fishes, with the net sinking the boats and provoking Peter to exclaim, "Depart from me; for I am a sinful man, O Lord," which should probably be translated, "I want no more of your miracles: natural fishing is good enough for my boats."

There are some other novelties in Luke's version. Pilate sends Jesus to Herod, who happens to be in Jerusalem just then, because Herod had expressed some curiosity about him; but nothing comes of it: the prisoner will not speak to him. When Jesus is ill received in a Samaritan village James and John propose to call down fire from heaven and destroy it; and Jesus replies that he is come not to destroy lives but to save them. The bias of Jesus against lawyers is emphasized, and also his resolution not to admit that he is more bound to his relatives than to strangers. He snubs a woman who blesses his mother. As this is contrary to the traditions of sentimental romance, Luke would presumably have avoided it had he not become persuaded that the brotherhood of Man and the Fatherhood of God are superior even to sentimental considerations. The story of the lawyer asking what are the two chief commandments is changed by making Jesus put the question to the lawyer instead of answering it.

As to doctrine, Luke is only clear when his feelings are touched. His logic is weak; for some of the sayings of Jesus are pieced together wrongly, as anyone who has read them in the right order and context in Matthew will discover at once. He does not make anything new out of Christ's mission, and, like the other evan-gelists, thinks that the whole point of it is that Jesus was the long expected Christ, and that he will presently come back to earth and establish his kingdom, having duly died and risen again after three days. Yet Luke not only records the teaching as to communism and the discarding of hate, which have, of course, nothing to do with the Second Coming, but quotes one very re-markable saying which is not compatible with it, which is, that people must not go about asking where the kingdom of heaven is, and saying "Lo, here!" and "Lo, there!" because the kingdom of heaven is within them. But Luke has no sense that this belongs to a quite different order of thought to his Christianity, and retains undisturbed his view of the kingdom as a locality as definite as Jerusalem or Madagascar.

JOHN

A NEW STORY AND A NEW CHARACTER

The gospel of John is a surprise after the others. Matthew, Mark, and Luke describe the same events in the same order (the variations in Luke are negligible), and their gospels are therefore called the synoptic gospels. They tell substantially the same story of a wandering preacher who at the end of his life came to Jerusalem. John describes a preacher who spent practically his whole adult life in the capital, with occasional visits to the provinces. His circumstantial account of the calling of Peter and the sons of Zebedee is quite different from the others; and he says nothing about their being fishermen. He says expressly that Jesus, though baptized by John, did not himself practise baptism, and that his disciples did. Christ's agonized appeal against his doom in the garden of Gethsemane becomes a cold-blooded suggestion made in the temple at a much earlier period. Jesus argues much more; complains a good deal of the unreasonableness and dislike with which he is met; is by no means silent before Caiaphas and Pilate; lays much greater stress on his resurrection and on the eating of his body (losing all his disciples except the twelve in consequence); says many apparently contradictory and nonsensical things to which no ordinary reader can now find any clue; and gives the impression of an educated, not to say sophisticated mystic, different both in character and schooling from the simple and downright preacher of Matthew and Mark, and the urbane easy-minded charmer of Luke. Indeed, the Jews say of him "How knoweth this man letters, having never learnt?"

John the Immortal Eye-Witness

John, moreover, claims to be not only a chronicler but a witness. He declares that he is "the disciple whom Jesus loved," and that he actually leaned on the bosom of Jesus at the last supper and asked in a whisper which of them it was that should betray him. Jesus whispered that he would give a sop to the traitor, and thereupon handed one to Judas, who ate it and immediately became possessed by the devil. This is more natural than the other accounts, in which Jesus openly indicates Judas without eliciting any protest or exciting any comment. It also implies that Jesus deliberately bewitched Judas in order to bring about his own betrayal. Later on John claims that Jesus said to Peter "If I will that John tarry til I come, what is that to thee?"; and John, with a rather obvious mock modesty, adds that he must not claim to be immortal, as the disciples concluded; for Christ did not use that expression, but merely remarked "If I will that he tarry til I come." No other evangelist claims personal intimacy with Christ, or even pretends to be his contemporary (there is no ground for identifying Matthew the publican with Matthew the Evangelist); and John is the only evangelist whose account of Christ's career and character is hopelessly irreconcilable with Matthew's. He is almost as bad as Matthew, by the way, in his repeated explanations of Christ's actions as having no other purpose than to fulfil the old prophecies. The impression is more unpleasant, because, as John, unlike Matthew, is educated, subtle, and obsessed with artificial intellectual mystifications, the discovery that he is stupid or superficial in so simple a matter strikes one with distrust and dislike, in spite of his great literary charm, a good example of which is his transfiguration of the harsh episode of the Syrophenician woman into the pleasant story of the woman of Samaria. This perhaps is why his claim to be John the disciple, or to be a contemporary of Christ or even of any survivor of Christ's generation, has been disputed, and finally, it seems, disallowed. But I repeat, I take no note here of the dis-

putes of experts as to the date of the gospels, not because I am
not acquainted with them, but because, as the earliest codices
are Greek manuscripts of the fourth century A.D., and the Syrian
ones are translations from the Greek, the paleographic expert has
no difficulty in arriving at whatever conclusion happens to suit
his beliefs or disbeliefs; and he never succeeds in convincing the
other experts except when they believe or disbelieve exactly as he
does. Hence I conclude that the dates of the original narratives
cannot be ascertained, and that we must make the best of the
evangelists' own accounts of themselves. There is, as we have
seen, a very marked difference between them, leaving no doubt
that we are dealing with four authors of well-marked diversity;
but they all end in an attitude of expectancy of the Second Coming which they agree in declaring Jesus to have positively and un-
equivocally promised within the lifetime of his contemporaries.
Any believer compiling a gospel after the last of these contemporaries had passed away, would either reject and omit the tradition of that promise on the ground that since it was not fulfilled,
and could never now be fulfilled, it could not have been made, or
else have had to confess to the Jews, who were the keenest critics
of the Christians, that Jesus was either an impostor or the victim
of a delusion. Now all the evangelists except Matthew expressly
declare themselves to be believers; and Matthew's narrative is
obviously not that of a sceptic. I therefore assume as a matter of
common sense that, interpolations apart, the gospels are derived
from narratives written in the first century A.D. I include John,
because though it may be claimed that he hedged his position by
claiming that Christ, who specially loved him, endowed him with
a miraculous life until the Second Coming, the conclusion being
that John is alive at this moment, I cannot believe that a literary
forger could hope to save the situation by so outrageous a pretension. Also, John's narrative is in many passages nearer to the
realities of public life than the simple chronicle of Matthew or the
sentimental romance of Luke. This may be because John was obviously more a man of the world than the others, and knew, as

mere chroniclers and romancers never know, what actually happens away from books and desks. But it may also be because he saw and heard what happened instead of collecting traditions about it. The paleographers and daters of first quotations may say what they please: John's claim to give evidence as an eyewitness whilst the others are only compiling history is supported by a certain verisimilitude which appeals to me as one who has preached a new doctrine and argued about it, as well as written stories. This verisimilitude may be dramatic art backed by knowledge of public life; but even at that we must not forget that the best dramatic art is the operation of a divinatory instinct for truth. Be that as it may, John was certainly not the man to believe in the Second Coming and yet give a date for it after that date had passed. There is really no escape from the conclusion that the originals of all the gospels date from the period within which there was still a possibility of the Second Coming occurring at the promised time.

THE PECULIAR THEOLOGY OF JESUS

In spite of the suspicions roused by John's idiosyncrasies, his narrative is of enormous importance to those who go to the gospels for a credible modern religion. For it is John who adds to the other records such sayings as that "I and my father are one"; that "God is a spirit"; that the aim of Jesus is not only that the people should have life, but that they should have it "more abundantly" (a distinction much needed by people who think a man is either alive or dead, and never consider the important question how much alive he is); and that men should bear in mind what they were told in the 82nd Psalm: that they are gods, and are responsible for the doing of the mercy and justice of God. The Jews stoned him for saying these things, and, when he remonstrated with them for stupidly stoning one who had done nothing to them but good works, replied "For a good work we stone thee not; but for blasphemy, because that thou, being a man, makest thyself God." He insists (referring to the 82nd Psalm) that if it is part of their own religion that they are gods on the assurance of God himself, it cannot be blasphemy for him, whom the Father sanctified and sent into the world, to say "I am the son of God." But they will not have this at any price; and he has to escape from their fury. Here the point is obscured by the distinction made by Jesus between himself and other men. He says, in effect, "If you are gods, then, *a fortiori*, I am a god." John makes him say this, just as he makes him say "I am the light of the world." But Matthew makes him say to the people "Ye are the light of the world." John has no grip of the significance of these scraps which he has picked up: he is far more interested in a notion of his own that men can escape death and do even more extraordinary things than Christ himself: in fact, he actually represents Jesus as promising this explicitly, and is finally led into the audacious hint that he, John, is himself immortal in the flesh. Still, he does not miss the significant sayings altogether. However inconsistent they may be with the doctrine he is consciously driving at, they appeal to some sub-intellectual instinct in him that makes him stick them in, like a child sticking tinsel stars on the robe of a toy angel.

John does not mention the ascension; and the end of his narrative leaves Christ restored to life, and appearing from time to time among his disciples. It is on one of these occasions that John describes the miraculous draught of fishes which Luke places at the other end of Christ's career, at the call of the sons of Zebedee.

John agreed as to the Trial and Crucifixion

Although John, following his practice of shewing Jesus's skill as a debater, makes him play a less passive part at his trial, he still gives substantially the same account of it as all the rest. And the question that would occur to any modern reader never occurs to him, any more than it occurred to Matthew, Mark, or Luke. That question is, Why on earth did not Jesus defend himself, and make the people rescue him from the High Priest? He was so popular that they were unable to prevent him driving the money-changers out of the temple, or to arrest him for it. When they did arrest him afterwards, they had to do it at night in a garden. He could have argued with them as he had often done in the temple, and justified himself both to the Jewish law and to Caesar. And he had physical force at his command to back up his arguments: all that was needed was a speech to rally his followers; and he was not gagged. The reply of the evangelists would have been that all these inquiries are idle, because if Jesus had wished to escape, he could have saved himself all that trouble by doing what John describes him as doing: that is, casting his captors to the earth by an exertion of his miraculous power. If you asked John why he let them get up again and torment and execute him, John would have replied that it was part of the destiny of God to be slain and buried and to rise again, and that to have avoided this destiny would have been to repudiate his Godhead. And that is the only apparent explanation. Whether you believe with the evangelists that Christ could have rescued himself by a miracle, or, as a modern Secularist, point out that he could have defended himself effectually, the fact remains that according to all the narratives he did not do so. He had to die like a god, not to save himself "like one of the princes."[1] The consensus on this point is important, because it proves the absolute sincerity of Jesus's declaration that he was a god. No impostor would have accepted such dreadful consequences without an effort to save himself. No impostor would have been nerved to endure them by the conviction that he would rise from the grave and live again after three days. If we accept the story at all, we must believe this, and

[1] Jesus himself had referred to that psalm (LXXXII) in which men who have judged unjustly and accepted the persons of the wicked (including by anticipation practically all the white inhabitants of the British Isles and the North American continent, to mention no other places) are condemned in the words, "I have said, ye are gods; and all of ye are children of the Most High; but ye shall die like men, and fall like one of the princes."

believe also that his promise to return in glory and establish his
kingdom on earth within the lifetime of men then living, was one
which he believed that he could, and indeed must fulfil. Two
evangelists declare that in his last agony he despaired, and reproached God for forsaking him. The other two represent him
as dying in unshaken conviction and charity with the simple
remark that the ordeal was finished. But all four testify that
his faith was not deceived, and that he actually rose again after
three days. And I think it unreasonable to doubt that all four
wrote their narratives in full faith that the other promise would
be fulfilled too, and that they themselves might live to witness
the Second Coming.

Credibility of the Gospels

It will be noted by the older among my readers, who are sure
to be obsessed more or less by elderly wrangles as to whether
the gospels are credible as matter-of-fact narratives, that I have
hardly raised this question, and have accepted the credible and
incredible with equal complacency. I have done this because
credibility is a subjective condition, as the evolution of religious
belief clearly shews. Belief is not dependent on evidence and
reason. There is as much evidence that the miracles occurred as
that the battle of Waterloo occurred, or that a large body of
Russian troops passed through England in 1914 to take part in
the war on the western front. The reasons for believing in the
murder of Pompey are the same as the reasons for believing in
the raising of Lazarus. Both have been believed and doubted by
men of equal intelligence. Miracles, in the sense of phenomena
we cannot explain, surround us on every hand: life itself is the
miracle of miracles. Miracles in the sense of events that violate
the normal course of our experience are vouched for every day:
the flourishing Church of Christ Scientist is founded on a multitude of such miracles. Nobody believes all the miracles: everybody believes some of them. I cannot tell why men who will not

D

believe that Jesus ever existed yet believe firmly that Shakespear was Bacon. I cannot tell why people who believe that angels appeared and fought on our side at the battle of Mons, and who believe that miracles occur quite frequently at Lourdes, nevertheless boggle at the miracle of the liquefaction of the blood of St Januarius, and reject it as a trick of priestcraft. I cannot tell why people who will not believe Matthew's story of three kings bringing costly gifts to the cradle of Jesus, believe Luke's story of the shepherds and the stable. I cannot tell why people, brought up to believe the Bible in the old literal way as an infallible record and revelation, and rejecting that view later on, begin by rejecting the Old Testament, and give up the belief in a brimstone hell before they give up (if they ever do) the belief in a heaven of harps, crowns, and thrones. I cannot tell why people who will not believe in baptism on any terms believe in vaccination with the cruel fanaticism of inquisitors. I am convinced that if a dozen sceptics were to draw up in parallel columns a list of the events narrated in the gospels which they consider credible and incredible respectively, their lists would be different in several particulars. Belief is literally a matter of taste.

FASHIONS IN BELIEF

Now matters of taste are mostly also matters of fashion. We are conscious of a difference between medieval fashions in belief and modern fashions. For instance, though we are more credulous than men were in the Middle Ages, and entertain such crowds of fortune-tellers, magicians, miracle workers, agents of communication with the dead, discoverers of the elixir of life, transmuters of metals, and healers of all sorts, as the Middle Ages never dreamed of as possible, yet we will not take our miracles in the form that convinced the Middle Ages. Arithmetical numbers appealed to the Middle Ages just as they do to us, because they are difficult to deal with, and because the greatest masters of numbers, the Newtons and Leibnitzes, rank among the greatest men.

But there are fashions in numbers too. The Middle Ages took a fancy to some familiar number like seven; and because it was an odd number, and the world was made in seven days, and there are seven stars in Charles's Wain, and for a dozen other reasons, they were ready to believe anything that had a seven or a seven times seven in it. Seven deadly sins, seven swords of sorrow in the heart of the Virgin, seven champions of Christendom, seemed obvious and reasonable things to believe in simply because they were seven. To us, on the contrary, the number seven is the stamp of superstition. We will believe in nothing less than millions. A medieval doctor gained his patient's confidence by telling him that his vitals were being devoured by seven worms. Such a diagnosis would ruin a modern physician. The modern physician tells his patient that he is ill because every drop of his blood is swarming with a million microbes; and the patient believes him abjectly and instantly. Had a bishop told William the Conqueror that the sun was seventy-seven miles distant from the earth, William would have believed him not only out of respect for the Church, but because he would have felt that seventy-seven miles was the proper distance. The Kaiser, knowing just as little about it as the Conqueror, would send that bishop to an asylum. Yet he (I presume) unhesitatingly accepts the estimate of ninety-two and nine-tenths millions of miles, or whatever the latest big figure may be.

CREDIBILITY AND TRUTH

And here I must remind you that our credulity is not to be measured by the truth of the things we believe. When men believed that the earth was flat, they were not credulous: they were using their common sense, and, if asked to prove that the earth was flat, would have said simply, "Look at it." Those who refuse to believe that it is round are exercising a wholesome scepticism. The modern man who believes that the earth is round is grossly credulous. Flat Earth men drive him to fury by confuting him with the greatest ease when he tries to argue about it. Confront him with a theory that the earth is cylindrical, or annular, or hour-glass shaped, and he is lost. The thing he believes may be true, but that is not why he believes it: he believes it because in some mysterious way it appeals to his imagination. If you ask him why he believes that the sun is ninety-odd million miles off, either he will have to confess that he doesnt know, or he will say that Newton proved it. But he has not read the treatise in which Newton proved it, and does not even know that it was written in Latin. If you press an Ulster Protestant as to why he regards Newton as an infallible authority, and St Thomas Aquinas or the Pope as superstitious liars whom, after his death, he will have the pleasure of watching from his place in heaven whilst they roast in eternal flame, or if you ask me why I take into serious consideration Colonel Sir Almroth Wright's estimates of the number of streptococci contained in a given volume of serum whilst I can only laugh at the earlier estimates of the number of angels that can be accommodated on the point of a needle, no reasonable reply is possible except that somehow sevens and angels are out of fashion, and billions and streptococci are all the rage. I simply cannot tell you why Bacon, Montaigne, and Cervantes had a quite different fashion of credulity and incredulity from the Venerable Bede and Piers Plowman and the divine doctors of the Aquinas-Aristotle school, who were certainly no stupider, and had the same facts before them. Still less can I explain why, if we assume that these leaders of thought had all reasoned out their beliefs, their authority seemed conclusive to one generation and blasphemous to another, neither generation having followed the reasoning or gone into the facts of the matter for itself at all.

It is therefore idle to begin disputing with the reader as to what he should believe in the gospels and what he should disbelieve. He will believe what he can, and disbelieve what he must. If he draws any lines at all, they will be quite arbitrary ones. St John tells us that when Jesus explicitly claimed divine honors by the sacrament of his body and blood, so many of his disciples left him that their number was reduced to twelve. Many modern readers will not hold out so long: they will give in at the first miracle. Others will discriminate. They will accept the healing miracles, and reject the feeding of the multitude. To some the walking on the water will be a legendary exaggeration of a swim, ending in an ordinary rescue of Peter; and the raising of Lazarus will be only a similar glorification of a commonplace feat of artificial respiration, whilst others will scoff at it as a planned imposture in which Lazarus acted as a confederate. Between the rejection of the stories as wholly fabulous and the acceptance of them as the evangelists themselves mean them to be accepted, there will be many shades of belief and disbelief, of sympathy and derision. It is not a question of being a Christian or not. A Mahometan Arab will accept literally and without question parts of the narrative which an English Archbishop has to reject or explain away; and many Theosophists and lovers of the wisdom of India, who never enter a Christian Church except as sightseers, will revel in parts of John's gospel which mean nothing to a pious matter-of-fact Bradford manufacturer. Every reader takes from the Bible what he can get. In submitting a précis of the gospel narratives I have not implied any estimate either of their credibility or of their truth. I have simply informed him or reminded him, as the case may be, of what those narratives tell us about their hero.

Christian Iconolatry and the Peril of the Iconoclast

I must now abandon this attitude, and make a serious draft on the reader's attention by facing the question whether, if and when the medieval and Methodist will-to-believe the Salvationist and miraculous side of the gospel narratives fails us, as it plainly has failed the leaders of modern thought, there will be anything left of the mission of Jesus: whether, in short, we may not throw the gospels into the waste-paper basket, or put them away on the fiction shelf of our libraries. I venture to reply that we shall be, on the contrary, in the position of the man in Bunyan's riddle who found that "the more he threw away, the more he had." We get rid, to begin with, of the idolatrous or iconographic worship of Christ. By this I mean literally that worship which is given to pictures and statues of him, and to finished and unalterable stories about him. The test of the prevalence of this is that if you speak or write of Jesus as a real live person, or even as a still active God, such worshippers are more horrified than Don Juan was when the statue stepped from its pedestal and came to supper with him. You may deny the divinity of Jesus; you may doubt whether he ever existed; you may reject Christianity for Judaism, Mahometanism, Shintoism, or Fire Worship; and the iconolaters, placidly contemptuous, will only classify you as a freethinker or a heathen. But if you venture to wonder how Christ would have looked if he had shaved and had his hair cut, or what size in shoes he took, or whether he swore when he stood on a nail in the carpenter's shop, or could not button his robe when he was in a hurry, or whether he laughed over the repartees by which he baffled the priests when they tried to trap him into sedition and blasphemy, or even if you tell any part of his story in the vivid terms of modern colloquial slang, you will produce an extraordinary dismay and horror among the iconolaters. You will have made the picture come out of its frame, the statue descend from its pedestal, the story become real, with all the incalculable consequences that may flow from this terrifying miracle. It is at such moments that you realize that the iconolaters have never for a moment conceived Christ as a real person who meant what he said, as a fact, as a force like electricity, only needing the invention of suitable political machinery to be applied to the affairs of mankind with revolutionary effect.

Thus it is not disbelief that is dangerous in our society: it is belief. The moment it strikes you (as it may any day) that Christ is not the lifeless harmless image he has hitherto been to you, but a rallying centre for revolutionary influences which all established States and Churches fight, you must look to yourselves; for you have brought the image to life; and the mob may not be able to bear that horror.

THE ALTERNATIVE TO BARABBAS

But mobs must be faced if civilization is to be saved. It did not need the present war to shew that neither the iconographic Christ nor the Christ of St Paul has succeeded in effecting the salvation of human society. Whilst I write, the Turks are said to be massacring the Armenian Christians on an unprecedented scale; but Europe is not in a position to remonstrate; for her Christians are slaying one another by every device which civilization has put within their reach as busily as they are slaying the Turks. Barabbas is triumphant everywhere; and the final use he makes of his triumph is to lead us all to suicide with heroic gestures and resounding lies. Now those who, like myself, see the Barabbasque social organization as a failure, and are convinced that the Life Force (or whatever you choose to call it) cannot be finally beaten by any failure, and will even supersede humanity by evolving a higher species if we cannot master the problems raised by the multiplication of our own numbers, have always known that Jesus had a real message, and have felt the fascination of his character and doctrine. Not that we should nowadays dream of claiming any supernatural authority for him, much less the technical authority which attaches to an educated modern philosopher and jurist. But when, having entirely got rid of Salvationist Christianity, and even contracted a prejudice against Jesus on the score of his involuntary connection with it, we engage on a purely scientific study of economics, criminology, and biology, and find that our practical conclusions are virtually those of Jesus, we are distinctly pleased and encouraged to find that we were doing him an injustice, and that the nimbus that surrounds his head in the pictures may be interpreted some day as a light of science rather than a declaration of sentiment or a label of idolatry.

The doctrines in which Jesus is thus confirmed are, roughly, the following:

1. The kingdom of heaven is within you. You are the son of God; and God is the son of man. God is a spirit, to be worshipped in spirit and in truth, and not an elderly gentleman to be bribed and begged from. We are members one of another; so that you cannot injure or help your neighbor without injuring or helping yourself. God is your father: you are here to do God's work; and you and your father are one.

2. Get rid of property by throwing it into the common stock. Dissociate your work entirely from money payments. If you let a child starve you are letting God starve. Get rid of all anxiety about tomorrow's dinner and clothes, because you cannot serve two masters: God and Mammon.

3. Get rid of judges and punishment and revenge. Love your neighbor as yourself, he being a part of yourself. And love your enemies: they are your neighbors.

4. Get rid of your family entanglements. Every mother you meet is as much your mother as the woman who bore you. Every man you meet is as much your brother as the man she bore after you. Dont waste your time at family funerals grieving for your relatives: attend to life, not to death: there are as good fish in the sea as ever came out of it, and better. In the kingdom of heaven, which, as aforesaid, is within you, there is no marriage nor giving in marriage, because you cannot devote your life to two divinities: God and the person you are married to.

Now these are very interesting propositions; and they become more interesting every day, as experience and science drive us more and more to consider them favorably. In considering them, we shall waste our time unless we give them a reasonable construction. We must assume that the man who saw his way through such a mass of popular passion and illusion as stands between us and a sense of the value of such teaching was quite aware of all the objections that occur to an average stockbroker in the first five minutes. It is true that the world is governed to a considerable extent by the considerations that occur to stockbrokers in the first five minutes; but as the result is that the world is so badly governed that those who know the truth can hardly bear to live in it, an objection from an average stockbroker constitutes in itself a *prima facie* case for any social reform.

THE REDUCTION TO MODERN PRACTICE OF CHRISTIANITY

All the same, we must reduce the ethical counsels and proposals of Jesus to modern practice if they are to be of any use to us. If we ask our stockbroker to act simply as Jesus advised his disciples to act, he will reply, very justly, "You are advising me to become a tramp." If we urge a rich man to sell all that he has and give it to the poor, he will inform us that such an operation is impossible. If he sells his shares and his lands, their purchaser will continue all those activities which oppress the poor. If all the rich men take the advice simultaneously the shares will fall to zero and the lands be unsaleable. If one man sells out and throws the money into the slums, the only result will be to add himself and his dependents to the list of the poor, and to do no good to the poor beyond giving a chance few of them a drunken spree. We must therefore bear in mind that whereas, in the time of Jesus, and in the ages which grew darker and darker after his death until the darkness, after a brief false dawn in the Reformation and the Renascence, culminated in the commercial night of the nineteenth century, it was believed that you could not make men good by Act of Parliament, we now know that you cannot make them good in any other way, and that a man who is better than his fellows is a nuisance. The rich man must sell up not only himself but his whole class; and that can be done only through the Chancellor of the Exchequer. The disciple cannot have his bread without money until there is bread for everybody without money; and that requires an elaborate municipal organization of the food supply, rate supported. Being members one of another means One Man One Vote, and One Woman One Vote, and universal suffrage and equal incomes and all sorts of modern political measures. Even in Syria in the time of Jesus his teachings could not possibly have been realized by a series of independent explosions of personal righteousness on the part of the separate units of the population. Jerusalem could not have done what even a village community cannot do, and what Robinson Crusoe himself could not have done if his conscience, and the stern compulsion of Nature, had not imposed a common rule on the half dozen Robinson Crusoes who struggled within him for not wholly compatible satisfactions. And what cannot be done in Jerusalem or Juan Fernandez cannot be done in London, New York, Paris, and Berlin.

In short, Christianity, good or bad, right or wrong, must perforce be left out of the question in human affairs until it is made practically applicable to them by complicated political devices; and to pretend that a field preacher under the governorship of Pontius Pilate, or even Pontius Pilate himself in council with all the wisdom of Rome, could have worked out applications of Christianity or any other system of morals for the twentieth century, is to shelve the subject much more effectually than Nero and all its other persecutors ever succeeded in doing. Personal righteousness, and the view that you cannot make people moral by Act of Parliament, is, in fact, the favorite defensive resort of the people who, consciously or subconsciously, are quite determined not to have their property meddled with by Jesus or any other reformer.

MODERN COMMUNISM

Now let us see what modern experience and sociology have to say to the suggestion of Jesus that you should get rid of your property by throwing it into the common stock. One can hear the Pharisees of Jerusalem and Chorazin and Bethsaida saying, "My good fellow, if you were to divide up the wealth of Judea equally today, before the end of the year you would have rich and poor, poverty and affluence, just as you have today; for there will always be the idle and the industrious, the thrifty and the wasteful, the drunken and the sober; and, as you yourself have very justly observed, the poor we shall have always with us." And we can hear the reply, "Woe unto you, liars and hypocrites; for ye have this very day divided up the wealth of the country yourselves, as must be done every day (for man liveth not otherwise than from hand to mouth, nor can fish and eggs endure for ever); and ye have divided it unjustly; also ye have said that my reproach to you for having the poor always with you was a law unto you that this evil should persist and stink in the nostrils of God to all eternity; wherefore I think that Lazarus will yet see you beside Dives in hell." Modern Capitalism has made short work of the primitive pleas for inequality. The Pharisees themselves have organized communism in capital. Joint stock is the order of the day. An attempt to return to individual properties as the basis of our production would smash civilization more completely than ten revolutions. You cannot get the fields tilled today until the farmer becomes a co-operator. Take the shareholder to his railway, and ask him to point out to you the particular length of rail, the particular seat in the railway carriage, the particular lever in the engine that is his very own and nobody elses; and he will shun you as a madman, very wisely. And if, like Ananias and Sapphira, you try to hold back your little shop or what not from the common stock, represented by the Trust, or Combine, or Kartel, the Trust will presently freeze you out and rope you in and finally strike you dead industrially as thoroughly as St Peter himself. There is no longer any practical question open as to Communism in production: the struggle today is over the distribution of the product: that is, over the daily dividing-up which is the first necessity of organized society.

REDISTRIBUTION

Now it needs no Christ to convince anybody today that our system of distribution is wildly and monstrously wrong. We have million-dollar babies side by side with paupers worn out by a long life of unremitted drudgery. One person in every five dies in a workhouse, a public hospital, or a madhouse. In cities like London the proportion is very nearly one in two. Naturally so outrageous a distribution has to be effected by violence pure and simple. If you demur, you are sold up. If you resist the selling up you are bludgeoned and imprisoned, the process being euphemistically called the maintenance of law and order. Iniquity can go no further. By this time nobody who knows the figures of the distribution defends them. The most bigoted British Conservative hesitates to say that his king should be much poorer than Mr Rockefeller, or to proclaim the moral superiority of prostitution to needlework on the ground that it pays better. The need for a drastic redistribution of income in all civilized countries is now as obvious and as generally admitted as the need for sanitation.

SHALL HE WHO MAKES, OWN?

It is when we come to the question of the proportions in which we are to redistribute that controversy begins. We are bewildered by an absurdly unpractical notion that in some way a man's income should be given to him, not to enable him to live, but as a sort of Sunday School Prize for good behavior. And this folly is complicated by a less ridiculous but quite as unpractical belief that it is possible to assign to each person the exact portion of the national income that he or she has produced. To a child it seems that the blacksmith has made a horse-shoe, and that therefore the horse-shoe is his. But the blacksmith knows that the horse-shoe does not belong solely to him, but to his landlord, to the rate collector and taxgatherer, to the men from whom he bought the iron and anvil and the coals, leaving only a scrap of its value for himself; and this scrap he has to exchange with the butcher and baker and the clothier for the things that he really appropriates as living tissue or its wrappings, paying for all of them more than their cost; for these fellow traders of his have also their landlords and moneylenders to satisfy. If, then, such simple and direct village examples of apparent individual production turn out on a moment's examination to be the products of an elaborate social organization, what is to be said of such products as dreadnoughts, factory-made pins and needles, and steel pens? If God takes the dreadnought in one hand and a steel pen in the other, and asks Job who made them, and to whom they should belong by maker's right, Job must scratch his puzzled head with a potsherd and be dumb, unless indeed it strikes him that God is the ultimate maker, and that all we have a right to do with the product is to feed his lambs.

LABOR TIME

So maker's right as an alternative to taking the advice of Jesus would not work. In practice nothing was possible in that direction but to pay a worker by labor time: so much an hour or day or week or year. But how much? When that question came up, the only answer was "as little as he can be starved into accepting," with the ridiculous results already mentioned, and the additional anomaly that the largest share went to the people who did not work at all, and the least to those who worked hardest. In England nine-tenths of the wealth goes into the pockets of one-tenth of the population.

THE DREAM OF DISTRIBUTION ACCORDING TO MERIT

Against this comes the protest of the Sunday School theorists "Why not distribute according to merit?" Here one imagines Jesus, whose smile has been broadening down the ages as attempt after attempt to escape from his teaching has led to deeper and deeper disaster, laughing outright. Was ever so idiotic a project mooted as the estimation of virtue in money? The London School of Economics is, we must suppose, to set examination papers with such questions as "Taking the money value of the virtues of Jesus as 100, and of Judas Iscariot as zero, give the correct figures for, respectively, Pontius Pilate, the proprietor of the Gadarene swine, the widow who put her mite in the poor-box, Mr Horatio Bottomley, Shakespear, Mr Jack Johnson, Sir Isaac Newton, Palestrina, Offenbach, Sir Thomas Lipton, Mr Paul Cinquevalli, your family doctor, Florence Nightingale, Mrs Siddons, your charwoman, the Archbishop of Canterbury, and the common hangman." Or "The late Mr Barney Barnato received as his lawful income three thousand times as much money as an English agricultural laborer of good general character. Name the principal virtues in which Mr Barnato exceeded the laborer three thousandfold; and give in figures the loss sustained by civilization when Mr Barnato was driven to despair and suicide by the reduction of his multiple to one thousand." The Sunday School idea, with its principle "to each the income he deserves," is really too silly for discussion. Hamlet disposed of it three hundred years ago. "Use every man after his deserts, and who shall scape whipping?" Jesus remains unshaken as the practical man; and we stand exposed as the fools, the blunderers, the unpractical visionaries. The moment you try to reduce the Sunday School idea to figures you find that it brings you back to the hopeless plan of paying for a man's time; and your examination paper will read "The time of Jesus was worth nothing (he complained that the foxes had holes and the birds of the air nests whilst he had not a place to lay his head). Dr Crippen's time was worth, say, three hundred and fifty pounds a year. Criticize this arrangement; and, if you dispute its justice, state in pounds, dollars, francs and marks, what their relative time wages ought to have been." Your answer may be that the question is in extremely bad taste and that you decline to answer it. But you cannot object to being asked how many minutes of a bookmaker's time are worth two hours of an astronomer's?

Vital Distribution

In the end you are forced to ask the question you should have asked at the beginning. What do you give a man an income for? Obviously to keep him alive. Since it is evident that the first condition on which he can be kept alive without enslaving somebody else is that he shall produce an equivalent for what it costs to keep him alive, we may quite rationally compel him to abstain from idling by whatever means we employ to compel him to abstain from murder, arson, forgery, or any other crime. The one supremely foolish thing to do with him is to do nothing: that is to be as idle, lazy, and heartless in dealing with him as he is in dealing with us. Even if we provided work for him instead of basing, as we do, our whole industrial system on successive competitive waves of overwork with their ensuing troughs of unemployment, we should still sternly deny him the alternative of not doing it; for the result must be that he will become poor and make his children poor if he has any; and poor people are cancers in the commonwealth, costing far more than if they were handsomely pensioned off as incurables. Jesus had more sense than to propose anything of the sort. He said to his disciples, in effect, "Do your work for love; and let the other people lodge and feed and clothe you for love." Or, as we should put it nowadays, "for nothing." All human experience and all natural uncommercialized human aspiration point to this as the right path. The Greeks said, "First secure an independent income; and then practise virtue." We all strive towards an independent income. We all know as well as Jesus did that if we have to take thought for the morrow as to whether there shall be anything to eat or drink it will be impossible for us to think of nobler things, or live a higher life than that of a mole, whose life is from beginning to end a frenzied pursuit of food. Until the community is organized in such a way that the fear of bodily want is forgotten as completely as the fear of wolves already is in civilized capitals, we shall never have a decent social life. Indeed the whole attraction of our present arrangement lies in the fact that it does relieve a handful of us from this fear; but as the relief is effected stupidly and wickedly by making the favored handful parasitic on the rest, they are smitten with the degeneracy which seems to be the inevitable biological penalty of complete parasitism. They corrupt culture and statecraft instead of contributing to them, their excessive leisure being as mischievous as the excessive toil of the laborers. Anyhow, the moral is clear. The two main problems of organized society: how to produce subsistence enough for all its members, and how to prevent the theft of that subsistence by idlers, should be carefully dissociated; for the triumphant solution of the first by our inventors and chemists has been offset by the disastrous failure of our rulers to solve the other. Optimism on this point is only wilful blindness: we all have the hard fact of the failure before us. The only people who cling to the lazy delusion that it is possible to find a just distribution that will work automatically are those who postulate some revolutionary change like land nationalization, which by itself would obviously only force into greater urgency the problem of how to distribute the product of the land among all the individuals in the community.

EQUAL DISTRIBUTION

When that problem is at last faced, the question of the proportion in which the national income shall be distributed can have only one answer. All our shares must be equal. It has always been so: it always will be so. It is true that the incomes of robbers vary considerably from individual to individual; and the variation is reflected in the incomes of their parasites. The commercialization of certain exceptional talents has also produced exceptional incomes, direct and derivative. Persons who live on rent of land and capital are economically, though not legally, in the category of robbers, and have grotesquely different incomes. But in the huge mass of mankind variation of income from individual to individual is unknown, because it is ridiculously impracticable.

As a device for persuading a carpenter that a judge is a creature
of superior nature to himself, to be deferred and submitted to
even to the death, we may give a carpenter a hundred pounds a
year and a judge five thousand; but the wage for one carpenter
is the wage for all the carpenters: the salary for one judge is the
salary for all the judges.

The Captain and the Cabin Boy

Nothing, therefore, is really in question, or ever has been, but
the differences between class incomes. Already there is economic
equality between captains, and economic equality between cabin
boys. What is at issue still is whether there shall be economic
equality between captains and cabin boys. What would Jesus
have said? Presumably he would have said that if your only
object is to produce a captain and a cabin boy for the purpose of
transferring you from Liverpool to New York, or to manœuvre
a fleet and carry powder from the magazine to the gun, then you
need give no more than a shilling to the cabin boy for every
pound you give to the more expensively trained captain. But if
in addition to this you desire to allow the two human souls which
are inseparable from the captain and the cabin boy, and which
alone differentiate them from the donkey-engine, to develop
all their possibilities, then you may find the cabin boy costing
rather more than the captain, because cabin boy's work does not
do so much for the soul as captain's work. Consequently you
will have to give him at least as much as the captain unless you
definitely wish him to be a lower creature, in which case the
sooner you are hanged as an abortionist the better. That is the
fundamental argument.

The Political and Biological Objections to Inequality

But there are other reasons for objecting to class stratification
of income which have heaped themselves up since the time of

E

Jesus. In politics it defeats every form of government except that of a necessarily corrupt oligarchy. Democracy in the most democratic modern republics: France and the United States for example, is an imposture and a delusion. It reduces justice and law to a farce: law becomes merely an instrument for keeping the poor in subjection; and accused workmen are tried, not by a jury of their peers, but by conspiracies of their exploiters. The press is the press of the rich and the curse of the poor: it becomes dangerous to teach men to read. The priest becomes the mere complement of the policeman in the machinery by which the countryhouse oppresses the village. Worst of all, marriage becomes a class affair: the infinite variety of choice which nature offers to the young in search of a mate is narrowed to a handful of persons of similar income; and beauty and health become the dreams of artists and the advertisements of quacks instead of the normal conditions of life. Society is not only divided but actually destroyed in all directions by inequality of income between classes: such stability as it has is due to the huge blocks of people between whom there is equality of income.

JESUS AS ECONOMIST

It seems therefore that we must begin by holding the right to an income as sacred and equal, just as we now begin by holding the right to life as sacred and equal. Indeed the one right is only a restatement of the other. To hang me for cutting a dock laborer's throat after making much of me for leaving him to starve when I do not happen to have a ship for him to unload is idiotic; for as he does far less mischief with his throat cut than when he is starving, a rational society would esteem the cutthroat more highly than the capitalist. The thing has become so obvious, and the evil so unendurable, that if our attempt at civilization is not to perish like all the previous ones, we shall have to organize our society in such a way as to be able to say to every person in the land, "Take no thought, saying What shall we eat? or What shall we drink? or Wherewithal shall we be clothed?" We shall then no longer have a race of men whose hearts are in their pockets and safes and at their bankers. As Jesus said, where your treasure is, there will your heart be also. That was why he recommended that money should cease to be a treasure, and that we should take steps to make ourselves utterly reckless of it, setting our minds free for higher uses. In other words, that we should all be gentlemen and take care of our country because our country takes care of us, instead of the commercialized cads we are, doing everything and anything for money, and selling our souls and bodies by the pound and the inch after wasting half the day haggling over the price. Decidedly, whether you think Jesus was God or not, you must admit that he was a first-rate political economist.

JESUS AS BIOLOGIST

He was also, as we now see, a first-rate biologist. It took a century and a half of evolutionary preachers, from Buffon and Goethe to Butler and Bergson, to convince us that we and our father are one; that as the kingdom of heaven is within us we need not go about looking for it and crying Lo here! and Lo there!; that God is not a picture of a pompous person in white robes in the family Bible, but a spirit; that it is through this spirit that we evolve towards greater abundance of life; that we are the lamps in which the light of the world burns: that, in short, we are gods though we die like men. All that is today sound biology and psychology; and the efforts of Natural Selectionists like Weismann to reduce evolution to mere automatism have not touched the doctrine of Jesus, though they have made short work of the theologians who conceived God as a magnate keeping men and angels as Lord Rothschild keeps buffaloes and emus at Tring.

MONEY THE MIDWIFE OF SCIENTIFIC COMMUNISM

It may be asked here by some simple-minded reader why we should not resort to crude Communism as the disciples were told to do. This would be quite practicable in a village where production was limited to the supply of the primitive wants which nature imposes on all human beings alike. We know that people need bread and boots without waiting for them to come and ask for these things and offer to pay for them. But when civilization advances to the point at which articles are produced that no man absolutely needs and that only some men fancy or can use, it is necessary that individuals should be able to have things made to their order and at their own cost. It is safe to provide bread for everybody because everybody wants and eats bread; but it would be absurd to provide microscopes and trombones, pet snakes and polo mallets, alembics and test tubes for everybody, as nine-tenths of them would be wasted; and the nine-tenths of the population who do not use such things would object to their being provided at all. We have in the invaluable instrument called money a means of enabling every individual to order and pay for the particular things he desires over and above the things he must consume in order to remain alive, plus the things the State insists on his having and using whether he wants to or not: for example, clothes, sanitary arrangements, armies and navies. In large communities, where even the most eccentric demands for manufactured articles average themselves out until they can be foreseen within a negligible margin of error, direct communism (Take what you want without payment, as the people do in Morris's News From Nowhere) will, after a little experience, be found not only practicable but highly economical to an extent that now seems impossible. The sportsmen, the musicians, the physicists, the biologists will get their apparatus for the asking as easily as their bread, or, as at present, their paving, street lighting, and bridges; and the deaf man will not object to contribute to communal flutes when the musician has to contribute to communal ear trumpets. There are cases (for example, radium) in which the demand may be limited to the merest handful of laboratory workers, and in which nevertheless the whole community must pay because the price is beyond the means of any individual worker. But even when the utmost allowance is made for extensions of communism that now seem fabulous, there will still remain for a long time to come regions of supply and demand in which men will need and use money or individual credit, and for which, therefore, they must have individual incomes. Foreign travel is an obvious instance. We are so far from even national communism still, that we shall probably have considerable developments of local communism before it becomes possible for a Manchester man to go up to London for a day without taking any money with him. The modern practical form of the communism of Jesus is therefore, for the present, equal distribution of the surplus of the national income that is not absorbed by simple communism.

JUDGE NOT

In dealing with crime and the family, modern thought and experience have thrown no fresh light on the views of Jesus. When Swift had occasion to illustrate the corruption of our civilization by making a catalogue of the types of scoundrels it produces, he always gave judges a conspicuous place alongside of them they judged. And he seems to have done this not as a restatement of the doctrine of Jesus, but as the outcome of his own observation and judgment. One of Mr Gilbert Chesterton's stories has for its hero a judge who, whilst trying a criminal case, is so overwhelmed by the absurdity of his position and the wickedness of the things it forces him to do, that he throws off the ermine there and then, and goes out into the world to live the life of an honest man instead of that of a cruel idol. There has also been a propaganda of a soulless stupidity called Determinism, representing man as a dead object driven hither and thither by his environment, antecedents, circumstances, and so forth, which nevertheless does remind us that there are limits to the number of cubits an individual can add to his stature morally or physically, and that it is silly as well as cruel to torment a man five feet high for not being able to pluck fruit that is within the reach of men of average height. I have known a case of an unfortunate child being beaten for not being able to tell the time after receiving an elaborate explanation of the figures on a clock dial, the fact being that she was short-sighted and could not see them. This is a typical illustration of the absurdities and cruelties into which we are led by the counter-stupidity to Determinism: the doctrine of Free Will. The notion that people can be good if they like, and that you should give them a powerful additional motive for goodness by tormenting them when they do evil, would soon reduce itself to absurdity if its application were not kept within the limits which nature sets to the self-control of most of us. Nobody supposes that a man with no ear for music or no mathematical faculty could be compelled on pain of death, however cruelly inflicted, to hum all the themes of Beethoven's symphonies or to complete Newton's work on fluxions.

LIMITS TO FREE WILL

Consequently such of our laws as are not merely the intimidations by which tyrannies are maintained under pretext of law, can be obeyed through the exercise of a quite common degree of reasoning power and self-control. Most men and women can endure the ordinary annoyances and disappointments of life without committing murderous assaults. They conclude therefore that any person can refrain from such assaults if he or she chooses to, and proceed to reinforce self-control by threats of severe punishment. But in this they are mistaken. There are people, some of them possessing considerable powers of mind and body, who can no more restrain the fury into which a trifling mishap throws them than a dog can restrain himself from snapping if he is suddenly and painfully pinched. People fling knives and lighted paraffin lamps at one another in a dispute over a dinner-table. Men who have suffered several long sentences of penal servitude for murderous assaults will, the very day after they are released, seize their wives and cast them under drays at an irritating word. We have not only people who cannot resist an opportunity of stealing for the sake of satisfying their wants, but even people who have a specific mania for stealing, and do it when they are in no need of the things they steal. Burglary fascinates some men as sailoring fascinates some boys. Among respectable people how many are there who can be restrained by the warnings of their doctors and the lessons of experience from eating and drinking more than is good for them? It is true that between self-controlled people and ungovernable people there is a narrow margin of moral malingerers who can be made to behave themselves by the fear of consequences; but it is not worth while maintaining an abominable system of malicious, deliberate, costly and degrading ill-treatment of criminals for the sake of these marginal cases. For practical dealing with crime, Determinism or Predestination is quite a good working rule. People without self-control enough for social purposes may be killed, or may be kept in asylums with a view to studying their condition and ascertaining whether it is curable. To torture them and give ourselves virtuous airs at their expense is ridiculous and barbarous; and the desire to do it is vindictive and cruel. And though vindictiveness and cruelty are at least human qualities when they are frankly proclaimed and indulged, they are loathsome when they assume the robes of Justice. Which, I take it, is why Shakespear's Isabella gave such a dressing-down to Judge Angelo, and why Swift reserved the hottest corner of his hell for judges. Also, of course, why Jesus said "Judge not that ye be not judged" and "If any man hear my words and believe not, I judge him not" because "he hath one that judgeth him": namely, the Father who is one with him.

When we are robbed we generally appeal to the criminal law, not considering that if the criminal law were effective we should not have been robbed. That convicts us of vengeance.

I need not elaborate the argument further. I have dealt with it sufficiently elsewhere. I have only to point out that we have been judging and punishing ever since Jesus told us not to; and I defy anyone to make out a convincing case for believing that the world has been any better than it would have been if there had never been a judge, a prison, or a gallows in it all that time. We have simply added the misery of punishment to the misery of crime, and the cruelty of the judge to the cruelty of the criminal. We have taken the bad man, and made him worse by torture and degradation, incidentally making ourselves worse in the process. It does not seem very sensible, does it? It would have been far easier to kill him as kindly as possible, or to label him and leave him to his conscience, or to treat him as an invalid or a lunatic is now treated (it is only of late years, by the way, that madmen have been delivered from the whip, the chain, and the cage); and this, I presume, is the form in which the teaching of Jesus could have been put into practice.

JESUS ON MARRIAGE AND THE FAMILY

When we come to marriage and the family, we find Jesus making the same objection to that individual appropriation of human beings which is the essence of matrimony as to the individual appropriation of wealth. A married man, he said, will try to please his wife, and a married woman to please her husband, instead of doing the work of God. This is another version of "Where your treasure is, there will your heart be also." Eighteen hundred years later we find a very different person from Jesus, Talleyrand to wit, saying the same thing. A married man with a family, said Talleyrand, will do anything for money. Now this, though not a scientifically precise statement, is true enough to be a moral objection to marriage. As long as a man has a right to risk his life or his livelihood for his ideas he needs only courage and conviction to make his integrity unassailable. But he forfeits that right when he marries. It took a revolution to rescue Wagner from his Court appointment at Dresden; and his wife never forgave him for being glad and feeling free when he lost it and threw her back into poverty. Millet might have gone on painting potboiling nudes to the end of his life if his wife had not been of a heroic turn herself. Women, for the sake of their children and parents, submit to slaveries and prostitutions that no unattached woman would endure.

This was the beginning and the end of the objection of Jesus to marriage and family ties, and the explanation of his conception of heaven as a place where there should be neither marrying nor giving in marriage. Now there is no reason to suppose that when he said this he did not mean it. He did not, as St Paul did afterwards in his name, propose celibacy as a rule of life; for he was not a fool, nor, when he denounced marriage, had he yet come to believe, as St Paul did, that the end of the world was at hand and there was therefore no more need to replenish the earth. He must have meant that the race should be continued without dividing with women and men the allegiance the individual owes to God within him. This raises the practical problem of how we are to secure the spiritual freedom and integrity of the priest and the nun without their barrenness and uncompleted experience. Luther the priest did not solve the problem by marrying a nun: he only testified in the most convincing and practical way to the fact that celibacy was a worse failure than marriage.

WHY JESUS DID NOT MARRY

To all appearance the problem oppresses only a few exceptional people. Thoroughly conventional women married to thoroughly conventional men should not be conscious of any restriction: the chain not only leaves them free to do whatever they want to do, but greatly facilitates their doing it. To them an attack on marriage is not a blow struck in defence of their freedom but at their rights and privileges. One would expect that they would not only demur vehemently to the teachings of Jesus in this matter, but object strongly to his not having been a married man himself. Even those who regard him as a god descended from his throne in heaven to take on humanity for a time might reasonably declare that the assumption of humanity must have been incomplete at its most vital point if he were a celibate. But the facts are flatly contrary. The mere thought of Jesus as a married man is felt to be blasphemous by the most conventional believers; and even those of us to whom Jesus is no supernatural personage, but a prophet only as Mahomet was a prophet, feel that there was something more dignified in the bachelordom of Jesus than in the spectacle of Mahomet lying distracted on the floor of his harem whilst his wives stormed and squabbled and henpecked round him. We are not surprised that when Jesus called the sons of Zebedee to follow him, he did not call their father, and that the disciples, like Jesus himself, were all men without family entanglements. It is evident from his impatience when people excused themselves from following him because of their family funerals, or when they assumed that his first duty was to his mother, that he had found family ties and domestic affections in his way at every turn, and had become persuaded at last that no man could follow his inner light until he was free from their compulsion. The absence of any protest against this tempts us to declare that on this question of marriage there are no conventional people; and that everyone of us is at heart a good Christian sexually.

INCONSISTENCY OF THE SEX INSTINCT

But the question is not so simple as that. Sex is an exceedingly subtle and complicated instinct; and the mass of mankind neither know nor care much about freedom of conscience, which is what Jesus was thinking about, and are concerned almost to obsession with sex, as to which Jesus said nothing. In our sexual natures we are torn by an irresistible attraction and an overwhelming repugnance and disgust. We have two tyrannous physical pas-

sions: concupiscence and chastity. We become mad in pursuit of
sex: we become equally mad in the persecution of that pursuit.
Unless we gratify our desire the race is lost: unless we restrain it
we destroy ourselves. We are thus led to devise marriage institutions which will at the same time secure opportunities for the
gratification of sex and raise up innumerable obstacles to it;
which will sanctify it and brand it as infamous; which will identify
it with virtue and with sin simultaneously. Obviously it is useless
to look for any consistency in such institutions; and it is only
by continual reform and readjustment, and by a considerable
elasticity in their enforcement, that a tolerable result can be
arrived at. I need not repeat here the long and elaborate examination of them that I prefixed to my play entitled Getting Married.
Here I am concerned only with the views of Jesus on the question;
and it is necessary, in order to understand the attitude of the
world towards them, that we should not attribute the general
approval of the decision of Jesus to remain unmarried as an
endorsement of his views. We are simply in a state of confusion
on the subject; but it is part of the confusion that we should
conclude that Jesus was a celibate, and shrink even from the idea
that his birth was a natural one, yet cling with ferocity to the
sacredness of the institution which provides a refuge from celibacy.

FOR BETTER FOR WORSE

Jesus, however, did not express a complicated view of marriage.
His objection to it was quite simple, as we have seen. He perceived
that nobody could live the higher life unless money and sexual
love were obtainable without sacrificing it; and he saw that the
effect of marriage as it existed among the Jews (and as it still
exists among ourselves) was to make the couples sacrifice every
higher consideration until they had fed and pleased one another.
The worst of it is that this dangerous preposterousness in marriage,
instead of improving as the general conduct of married couples
improves, becomes much worse. The selfish man to whom his

wife is nothing but a slave, the selfish woman to whom her husband is nothing but a scapegoat and a breadwinner, are not held back from spiritual or any other adventures by fear of their effect on the welfare of their mates. Their wives do not make recreants and cowards of them: their husbands do not chain them to the cradle and the cooking range when their feet should be beautiful on the mountains. It is precisely as people become more kindly, more conscientious, more ready to shoulder the heavier part of the burden (which means that the strong shall give way to the weak and the slow hold back the swift), that marriage becomes an intolerable obstacle to individual evolution. And that is why the revolt against marriage of which Jesus was an exponent always recurs when civilization raises the standard of marital duty and affection, and at the same time produces a greater need for individual freedom in pursuit of a higher evolution.

THE REMEDY

This, fortunately, is only one side of marriage; and the question arises, can it not be eliminated? The reply is reassuring: of course it can. There is no mortal reason in the nature of things why a married couple should be economically dependent on one another. The Communism advocated by Jesus, which we have seen to be entirely practicable, and indeed inevitable if our civilization is to be saved from collapse, gets rid of that difficulty completely. And with the economic dependence will go the force of the outrageous claims that derive their real sanction from the economic pressure behind them. When a man allows his wife to turn him from the best work he is capable of doing, and to sell his soul at the highest commercial prices obtainable; when he allows her to entangle him in a social routine that is wearisome and debilitating to him, or tie him to her apron strings when he needs that occasional solitude which is one of the most sacred of human rights, he does so because he has no right to impose eccentric standards of expenditure and unsocial habits on her, and because these conditions have produced by their pressure so general a custom of chaining wedded couples to one another that married people are coarsely derided when their partners break the chain. And when a woman is condemned by her parents to wait in genteel idleness and uselessness for a husband when all her healthy social instincts call her to acquire a profession and work, it is again her economic dependence on them that makes their tyranny effective.

THE CASE FOR MARRIAGE

Thus, though it would be too much to say that everything that is obnoxious in marriage and family life will be cured by Communism, yet it can be said that it will cure what Jesus objected to in these institutions. He made no comprehensive study of them: he only expressed his own grievance with an overwhelming sense that it is a grievance so deep that all the considerations on the other side are as dust in the balance. Obviously there are such considerations, and very weighty ones too. When Talleyrand said that a married man with a family is capable of anything, he meant anything evil; but an optimist may declare, with equal half truth, that a married man is capable of anything good; that marriage turns vagabonds into steady citizens; and that men and women will, for love of their mates and children, practise virtues that unattached individuals are incapable of. It is true that too much of this domestic virtue is self-denial, which is not a virtue at all; but then the following of the inner light at all costs is largely self-indulgence, which is just as suicidal, just as weak, just as cowardly as self-denial. Ibsen, who takes us into the matter far more resolutely than Jesus, is unable to find any golden rule: both Brand and Peer Gynt come to a bad end; and though Brand does not do as much mischief as Peer, the mischief he does do is of extraordinary intensity.

Celibacy no Remedy

We must, I think, regard the protest of Jesus against marriage and family ties as the claim of a particular kind of individual to be free from them because they hamper his own work intolerably. When he said that if we are to follow him in the sense of taking up his work we must give up our family ties, he was simply stating a fact; and to this day the Roman Catholic priest, the Buddhist lama, and the fakirs of all the eastern denominations accept the saying. It is also accepted by the physically enterprising, the explorers, the restlessly energetic of all kinds: in short, by the adventurous. The greatest sacrifice in marriage is the sacrifice of the adventurous attitude towards life: the being settled. Those who are born tired may crave for settlement; but to fresher and stronger spirits it is a form of suicide.

Now to say of any institution that it is incompatible with both the contemplative and adventurous life is to disgrace it so vitally that all the moralizings of all the Deans and Chapters cannot reconcile our souls to its slavery. The unmarried Jesus and the unmarried Beethoven, the unmarried Joan of Arc, Clare, Teresa, Florence Nightingale seem as they should be; and the saying that there is always something ridiculous about a married philosopher becomes inevitable. And yet the celibate is still more ridiculous than the married man: the priest, in accepting the alternative of celibacy, disables himself; and the best priests are those who have been men of this world before they became men of the world to come. But as the taking of vows does not annul an existing marriage, and a married man cannot become a priest, we are again confronted with the absurdity that the best priest is a reformed rake. Thus does marriage, itself intolerable, thrust us upon intolerable alternatives. The practical solution is to make the individual economically independent of marriage and the family, and to make marriage as easily dissoluble as any other partnership: in other words, to accept the conclusions to which experience is slowly driving both our sociologists and our legislators. This will not instantly cure all the evils of marriage, nor root up at one stroke its detestable tradition of property in human bodies. But it will leave Nature free to effect a cure; and in free soil the root may wither and perish.

This disposes of all the opinions and teachings of Jesus which are still matters of controversy. They are all in line with the best modern thought. He told us what we have to do; and we have had to find the way to do it. Most of us are still, as most were in his own time, extremely recalcitrant, and are being forced along that way by painful pressure of circumstances, protesting at every step that nothing will induce us to go; that is a ridiculous way, a disgraceful way, a socialistic way, an atheistic way, an immoral way, and that the vanguard ought to be ashamed of themselves and must be made to turn back at once. But they find that they have to follow the vanguard all the same if their lives are to be worth living.

AFTER THE CRUCIFIXION

Let us now return to the New Testament narrative; for what happened after the disappearance of Jesus is instructive. Unfortunately, the crucifixion was a complete political success. I remember that when I described it in these terms once before, I greatly shocked a most respectable newspaper in my native town, the Dublin Daily Express, because my journalistic phrase shewed that I was treating it as an ordinary event like Home Rule or the Insurance Act: that is (though this did not occur to the editor), as a real event which had really happened, instead of a portion of the Church service. I can only repeat, assuming as I am that it *was* a real event and did actually happen, that it was as complete a success as any in history. Christianity as a specific doctrine was slain with Jesus, suddenly and utterly. He was hardly cold in his grave, or high in his heaven (as you please), before the apostles dragged the tradition of him down to the level of the thing it has remained ever since. And that thing the intelligent heathen may study, if they would be instructed in it by modern books, in Samuel Butler's novel, The Way of All Flesh.

THE VINDICTIVE MIRACLES AND THE STONING OF STEPHEN

Take, for example, the miracles. Of Jesus alone of all the Christian miracle workers there is no record, except in certain gospels that all men reject, of a malicious or destructive miracle. A barren fig-tree was the only victim of his anger. Every one of his miracles on sentient subjects was an act of kindness. John declares that he healed the wound of the man whose ear was cut off (by Peter, John says) at the arrest in the garden. One of the first things the apostles did with their miraculous power was to strike dead a wretched man and his wife who had defrauded them by holding back some money from the common stock. They struck people blind or dead without remorse, judging because they had been judged. They healed the sick and raised the dead apparently in a spirit of pure display and advertisement. Their doctrine did not contain a ray of that light which reveals Jesus as one of the redeemers of men from folly and error. They cancelled him, and went back straight to John the Baptist and his formula of securing remission of sins by repentance and the rite of baptism (being born again of water and the spirit). Peter's first harangue softens us by the human touch of its exordium, which was a quaint assurance to his hearers that they must believe him to be sober because it was too early in the day to get drunk; but of Jesus he had nothing to say except that he was the Christ foretold by the prophets as coming from the seed of David, and that they must believe this and be baptized. To this the other apostles added incessant denunciations of the Jews for having crucified him, and threats of the destruction that would overtake them if they did not repent: that is, if they did not join the sect which the apostles were now forming. A quite intolerable young speaker named Stephen delivered an oration to the council, in which he first inflicted on them a tedious sketch of the history of Israel, with which they were presumably as well acquainted as he, and then reviled them in the most insulting terms as "stiffnecked and uncircumcized." Finally, after boring and annoying them to the utmost bearable extremity, he looked up and declared that he saw the heavens open, and Christ standing on the right hand of God. This was too much: they threw him out of the city and stoned him to death. It was a severe way of suppressing a tactless and conceited bore; but it was pardonable and human in comparison to the slaughter of poor Ananias and Sapphira.

Paul

Suddenly a man of genius, Paul, violently anti-Christian, enters on the scene, holding the clothes of the men who are stoning Stephen. He persecutes the Christians with great vigor, a sport which he combines with the business of a tentmaker. This temperamental hatred of Jesus, whom he has never seen, is a pathological symptom of that particular sort of conscience and nervous constitution which brings its victims under the tyranny of two delirious terrors: the terror of sin and the terror of death, which may be called also the terror of sex and the terror of life. Now Jesus, with his healthy conscience on his higher plane, was free from these terrors. He consorted freely with sinners, and was never concerned for a moment, as far as we know, about whether his conduct was sinful or not; so that he has forced us to accept him as the man without sin. Even if we reckon his last days as the days of his delusion, he none the less gave a fairly convincing exhibition of superiority to the fear of death. This must have both fascinated and horrified Paul, or Saul, as he was first called. The horror accounts for his fierce persecution of the Christians. The fascination accounts for the strangest of his fancies: the fancy for attaching the name of Jesus Christ to the great idea which flashed upon him on the road to Damascus, the idea that he could not only make a religion of his two terrors, but that the movement started by Jesus offered him the nucleus for his new Church. It

F

was a monstrous idea; and the shock of it, as he afterwards declared, struck him blind for days. He heard Jesus calling to him from the clouds, "Why persecute me?" His natural hatred of the teacher for whom Sin and Death had no terrors turned into a wild personal worship of him which has the ghastliness of a beautiful thing seen in a false light.

The chronicler of the Acts of the Apostles sees nothing of the significance of this. The great danger of conversion in all ages has been that when the religion of the high mind is offered to the lower mind, the lower mind, feeling its fascination without understanding it, and being incapable of rising to it, drags it down to its level by degrading it. Years ago I said that the conversion of a savage to Christianity is the conversion of Christianity to savagery. The conversion of Paul was no conversion at all: it was Paul who converted the religion that has raised one man above sin and death into a religion that delivered millions of men so completely into their dominion that their own common nature became a horror to them, and the religious life became a denial of life. Paul had no intention of surrendering either his Judaism or his Roman citizenship to the new moral world (as Robert Owen called it) of Communism and Jesuism. Just as in our own time Karl Marx, not content to take political economy as he found it, insisted on rebuilding it from the bottom upwards in his own way, and thereby gave a new lease of life to the errors it was just outgrowing, so Paul reconstructed the old Salvationism from which Jesus had vainly tried to redeem him, and produced a fantastic theology which is still the most amazing thing of the kind known to us. Being intellectually an inveterate Roman Rationalist, always discarding the irrational real thing for the unreal but ratiocinable postulate, he began by discarding Man as he is, and substituted a postulate which he called Adam. And when he was asked, as he surely must have been in a world not wholly mad, what had become of the natural man, he replied "Adam *is* the natural man." This was confusing to simpletons, because according to tradition Adam was certainly the name of the natural man as created in the garden of Eden. It was as if a preacher of our own time had described as typically British Frankenstein's monster, and called him Smith, and somebody, on demanding what about the man in the street, had been told "Smith *is* the man in the street." The thing happens often enough; for indeed the world is full of these Adams and Smiths and men in the street and average sensual men and economic men and womanly women and what not, all of them imaginary Atlases carrying imaginary worlds on their unsubstantial shoulders.

The Eden story provided Adam with a sin: the "original sin" for which we are all damned. Baldly stated, this seems ridiculous; nevertheless it corresponds to something actually existent not only in Paul's consciousness but in our own. The original sin was not the eating of the forbidden fruit, but the consciousness of sin which the fruit produced. The moment Adam and Eve tasted the apple they found themselves ashamed of their sexual relation, which until then had seemed quite innocent to them; and there is no getting over the hard fact that this shame, or state of sin, has persisted to this day, and is one of the strongest of our instincts. Thus Paul's postulate of Adam as the natural man was pragmatically true: it worked. But the weakness of Pragmatism is that most theories will work if you put your back into making them work, provided they have some point of contact with human nature. Hedonism will pass the pragmatic test as well as Stoicism. Up to a certain point every social principle that is not absolutely idiotic works: Autocracy works in Russia and Democracy in America; Atheism works in France, Polytheism in India, Monotheism throughout Islam, and Pragmatism, or No-ism, in England. Paul's fantastic conception of the damned Adam, represented by Bunyan as a pilgrim with a great burden of sins on his back, corresponded to the fundamental condition of evolution, which is, that life, including human life, is continually evolving, and must therefore be continually ashamed of itself and its present and past. Bunyan's pilgrim wants to get rid of his bundle of sins; but he also wants to reach "yonder shining light"; and when at last his bundle falls off him into the sepulchre of Christ, his pilgrimage is still unfinished and his hardest trials still ahead of him. His conscience remains uneasy; "original sin" still torments him; and his adventure with Giant Despair, who throws him into the dungeon of Doubting Castle, from which he escapes by the use of a skeleton key, is more terrible than any he met whilst the bundle was still on his back. Thus Bunyan's allegory of human nature breaks through the Pauline theology at a hundred points. His theological allegory, The Holy War, with its troops of Election Doubters, and its cavalry of "those that rode Reformadoes," is, as a whole, absurd, impossible, and, except in passages where the artistic old Adam momentarily got the better of the Salvationist theologian, hardly readable.

Paul's theory of original sin was to some extent idiosyncratic. He tells us definitely that he finds himself quite well able to avoid the sinfulness of sex by practising celibacy; but he recognizes, rather contemptuously, that in this respect he is not as other men are, and says that they had better marry than burn, thus admitting that though marriage may lead to placing the desire to please wife or husband before the desire to please God, yet preoccupation with unsatisfied desire may be even more ungodly than preoccupation with domestic affection. This view of the case inevitably led him to insist that a wife should be rather a slave than a partner, her real function being, not to engage a man's love and loyalty, but on the contrary to release them for God by relieving the man of all preoccupation with sex just as in her capacity of housekeeper and cook she relieves his preoccupation with hunger by the simple expedient of satisfying his appetite. This slavery also justifies itself pragmatically by working effectively; but it has made Paul the eternal enemy of Woman. Incidentally it has led to many foolish surmises about Paul's personal character and circumstances, by people so enslaved by sex that a celibate appears to them a sort of monster. They forget that not only whole priesthoods, official and unofficial, from Paul to Carlyle and Ruskin, have defied the tyranny of sex, but immense numbers of ordinary citizens of both sexes have, either voluntarily or under pressure of circumstances easily surmountable, saved their energies for less primitive activities.

Howbeit, Paul succeeded in stealing the image of Christ crucified for the figure-head of his Salvationist vessel, with its Adam posing as the natural man, its doctrine of original sin, and its damnation avoidable only by faith in the sacrifice of the cross. In fact, no sooner had Jesus knocked over the dragon of superstition than Paul boldly set it on its legs again in the name of Jesus.

THE CONFUSION OF CHRISTENDOM

Now it is evident that two religions having such contrary effects on mankind should not be confused as they are under a common name. There is not one word of Pauline Christianity in the characteristic utterances of Jesus. When Saul watched the clothes of the men who stoned Stephen, he was not acting upon beliefs which Paul renounced. There is no record of Christ's having ever said to any man: "Go and sin as much as you like: you can put it all on me." He said "Sin no more," and insisted that he was putting up the standard of conduct, not debasing it, and that the righteousness of the Christian must exceed that of the Scribe and Pharisee. The notion that he was shedding his blood in order that every petty cheat and adulterator and libertine might wallow in it and come out whiter than snow, cannot be imputed to him on his own authority. "I come as an infallible patent medicine for bad consciences" is not one of the sayings in the gospels. If Jesus could have been consulted on Bunyan's allegory as to that business of the burden of sin dropping from the pilgrim's back when he caught sight of the cross, we must infer from his teaching that he would have told Bunyan in forcible terms that he had never made a greater mistake in his life, and that the business of a Christ was to make self-satisfied sinners feel the burden of their sins and stop committing them instead of assuring them that they could not help it, as it was all Adam's fault, but that it did not matter as long as they were credulous and friendly about himself. Even when he believed himself to be a god, he did not regard himself as a scapegoat. He was to take away the sins of the world by good government, by justice and mercy, by setting the welfare of little children above the pride of princes, by casting all the quackeries and idolatries which now usurp and malversate the power of God into what our local authorities quaintly call the dust destructor, and by riding on the clouds of heaven in glory instead of in a thousand-guinea motor car. That was delirious, if you like; but it was the delirium of a free soul, not of a shame-bound one like Paul's. There has really never been a more monstrous imposition perpetrated than the imposition of the limitations of Paul's soul upon the soul of Jesus.

THE SECRET OF PAUL'S SUCCESS

Paul must soon have found that his followers had gained peace of mind and victory over death and sin at the cost of all moral responsibility; for he did his best to reintroduce it by making good conduct the test of sincere belief, and insisting that sincere belief was necessary to salvation. But as his system was rooted in the plain fact that as what he called sin includes sex and is therefore an ineradicable part of human nature (why else should Christ have had to atone for the sin of all future generations?) it was impossible for him to declare that sin, even in its wickedest extremity, could forfeit the sinner's salvation if he repented and believed. And to this day Pauline Christianity is, and owes its enormous vogue to being, a premium on sin. Its consequences have had to be held in check by the worldlywise majority through a violently anti-Christian system of criminal law and stern morality. But of course the main restraint is human nature, which has good impulses as well as bad ones, and refrains from theft and murder and cruelty, even when it is taught that it can commit them all at the expense of Christ and go happily to heaven after-

wards, simply because it does not always want to murder or rob
or torture.

It is now easy to understand why the Christianity of Jesus
failed completely to establish itself politically and socially, and
was easily suppressed by the police and the Church, whilst Paul-
inism overran the whole western civilized world, which was at
that time the Roman Empire, and was adopted by it as its official
faith, the old avenging gods falling helplessly before the new
Redeemer. It still retains, as we may see in Africa, its power of
bringing to simple people a message of hope and consolation that
no other religion offers. But this enchantment is produced by its
spurious association with the personal charm of Jesus, and exists
only for untrained minds. In the hands of a logical Frenchman
like Calvin, pushing it to its utmost conclusions, and devising
"institutes" for hardheaded adult Scots and literal Swiss, it becomes the most infernal of fatalisms; and the lives of civilized
children are blighted by its logic whilst negro piccaninnies are re-
joicing in its legends.

Paul's Qualities

Paul, however, did not get his great reputation by mere imposition and reaction. It is only in comparison with Jesus (to
whom many prefer him) that he appears common and conceited. Though in The Acts he is only a vulgar revivalist, he
comes out in his own epistles as a genuine poet, though by flashes
only. He is no more a Christian than Jesus was a Baptist: he is a
disciple of Jesus only as Jesus was a disciple of John. He does
nothing that Jesus would have done, and says nothing that Jesus
would have said, though much, like the famous ode to charity,
that he would have admired. He is more Jewish than the Jews,
more Roman than the Romans, proud both ways, full of startling
confessions and self-revelations that would not surprise us if they
were slipped into the pages of Nietzsche, tormented by an intellectual conscience that demanded an argued case even at the cost
of sophistry, with all sorts of fine qualities and occasional illu-

minations, but always hopelessly in the toils of Sin, Death, and Logic, which had no power over Jesus. As we have seen, it was by introducing this bondage and terror of his into the Christian doctrine that he adapted it to the Church and State systems which Jesus transcended, and made it practicable by destroying the specifically Jesuist side of it. He would have been quite in his place in any modern Protestant State; and he, not Jesus, is the true head and founder of our Reformed Church, as Peter is of the Roman Church. The followers of Paul and Peter made Christendom, whilst the Nazarenes were wiped out.

THE ACTS OF THE APOSTLES

Here we may return to the narrative called The Acts of the Apostles, which we left at the point where the stoning of Stephen was followed by the introduction of Paul. The author of The Acts, though a good story-teller, like Luke, was (herein also like Luke) much weaker in power of thought than in imaginative literary art. Hence we find Luke credited with the authorship of The Acts by people who like stories and have no aptitude for theology, whilst the book itself is denounced as spurious by Pauline theologians because Paul, and indeed all the apostles, are represented in it as very commonplace revivalists, interesting us by their adventures more than by any qualities of mind or character. Indeed, but for the epistles, we should have a very poor opinion of the apostles. Paul in particular is described as setting a fashion which has remained in continual use to this day. Whenever he addresses an audience, he dwells with great zest on his misdeeds before his pseudo conversion, with the effect of throwing into stronger relief his present state of blessedness; and he tells the story of that conversion over and over again, ending with exhortations to the hearers to come and be saved, and threats of the wrath that will overtake them if they refuse. At any revival meeting today the same thing may be heard, followed by the same conversions. This is natural enough; but it is totally unlike the preaching of Jesus, who never talked about his personal history, and never "worked up" an audience to hysteria. It aims at a purely nervous effect; it brings no enlightenment; the most ignorant man has only to become intoxicated with his own vanity, and mistake his self-satisfaction for the Holy Ghost, to become qualified as an apostle; and it has absolutely nothing to do with the characteristic doctrines of Jesus. The Holy Ghost may be at work all round producing wonders of art and science, and strengthening men to endure all sorts of martyrdoms for the enlargement of knowledge, and the enrichment and intensification of life ("that ye may have life more abundantly"); but the apostles, as described in The Acts, take no part in the struggle except as persecutors and revilers. To this day, when their successors get the upper hand, as in Geneva (Knox's "perfect city of Christ") and in Scotland and Ulster, every spiritual activity but moneymaking and churchgoing is stamped out; heretics are ruthlessly persecuted; and such pleasures as money can purchase are suppressed so that its possessors are compelled to go on making money because there is nothing else to do. And the compensation for all this privation is partly an insane conceit of being the elect of God, with a reserved seat in heaven, and partly, since even the most infatuated idiot cannot spend his life admiring himself, the less innocent excitement of punishing other people for not admiring him, and the nosing out of the sins of the people who, being intelligent enough to be incapable of mere dull self-righteousness, and highly susceptible to the beauty and interest of the real workings of the Holy Ghost, try to live more rational and abundant lives. The abominable amusement of terrifying children with threats of hell is another of these diversions, and perhaps the vilest and most mischievous of them. The net result is that the imitators of the apostles, whether they are called Holy Willies or Stigginses in derision, or, in admiration, Puritans or saints, are, outside their own congregations, and to a considerable extent inside them, heartily detested. Now nobody detests Jesus, though many who have been tormented in their childhood in his name include him in their general loathing of everything connected with the word religion; whilst others, who know him only by misrepresentation as a sentimental pacifist and an ascetic, include him in their general dislike of that type of character. In the same way a student who has had to "get up" Shakespear as a college subject may hate Shakespear; and people who dislike the theatre may include Molière in that dislike without ever having read a line of his or witnessed one of his plays; but nobody with any knowledge of Shakespear or Molière could possibly detest them, or read without pity and horror a description of their being insulted, tortured, and killed. And the same is true of Jesus. But it requires the most strenuous effort of conscience to refrain from crying "Serve him right" when we read of the stoning of Stephen; and nobody has ever cared twopence about the martyrdom of Peter: many better men have died worse deaths: for example, honest Hugh Latimer, who was burned by us, was worth fifty Stephens and a dozen Peters. One feels at last that when Jesus called Peter from his boat, he spoiled an honest fisherman, and made nothing better out of the wreck than a salvation monger.

The Controversies on Baptism and Transubstantiation

Meanwhile the inevitable effect of dropping the peculiar doctrines of Jesus and going back to John the Baptist, was to make it much easier to convert Gentiles than Jews; and it was by following the line of least resistance that Paul became the apostle to the Gentiles. The Jews had their own rite of initiation: the rite of circumcision; and they were fiercely jealous for it, because it marked them as the chosen people of God, and set them apart from the Gentiles, who were simply the uncircumcized. When Paul, finding that baptism made way faster among the Gentiles than among the Jews, as it enabled them to plead that they too were sanctified by a rite of later and higher authority than the Mosaic rite, he was compelled to admit that circumcision did not matter; and this, to the Jews, was an intolerable blasphemy. To

Gentiles like ourselves, a good deal of the Epistle to the Romans
is now tedious to unreadableness because it consists of a hopeless
attempt by Paul to evade the conclusion that if a man were baptized it did not matter a rap whether he was circumcized or not.
Paul claims circumcision as an excellent thing in its way for a
Jew; but if it has no efficacy towards salvation, and if salvation is
the one thing needful—and Paul was committed to both propositions—his pleas in mitigation only made the Jews more determined to stone him.

Thus from the very beginning of apostolic Christianity, it was
hampered by a dispute as to whether salvation was to be attained
by a surgical operation or by a sprinkling of water: mere rites on
which Jesus would not have wasted twenty words. Later on,
when the new sect conquered the Gentile west, where the dispute
had no practical application, the other ceremony—that of eating
the god—produced a still more disastrous dispute, in which a
difference of belief, not as to the obligation to perform the ceremony, but as to whether it was a symbolic or a real ingestion of
divine substance, produced persecution, slaughter, hatred, and
everything that Jesus loathed, on a monstrous scale.

But long before that, the superstitions which had fastened on
the new faith made trouble. The parthenogenetic birth of Christ,
simple enough at first as a popular miracle, was not left so simple
by the theologians. They began to ask of what substance Christ
was made in the womb of the virgin. When the Trinity was added
to the faith the question arose, was the virgin the mother of God
or only the mother of Jesus? Arian schisms and Nestorian schisms
arose on these questions; and the leaders of the resultant agita-
tions rancorously deposed one another and excommunicated one
another according to their luck in enlisting the emperors on their
side. In the IV century they began to burn one another for differences of opinion in such matters. In the VIII century Charlemagne made Christianity compulsory by killing those who refused to embrace it; and though this made an end of the voluntary
character of conversion, Charlemagne may claim to be the first

Christian who put men to death for any point of doctrine that really mattered. From his time onward the history of Christian controversy reeks with blood and fire, torture and warfare. The Crusades, the persecutions in Albi and elsewhere, the Inquisition, the "wars of religion" which followed the Reformation, all presented themselves as Christian phenomena; but who can doubt that they would have been repudiated with horror by Jesus? Our own notion that the massacre of St Bartholomew's was an outrage on Christianity, whilst the campaigns of Gustavus Adolphus, and even of Frederick the Great, were a defence of it, is as absurd as the opposite notion that Frederick was Antichrist, and Torquemada and Ignatius Loyola men after the very heart of Jesus. Neither they nor their exploits had anything to do with him. It is probable that Archbishop Laud and John Wesley died equally persuaded that he in whose name they had made themselves famous on earth would receive them in Heaven with open arms. George Fox the Quaker would have had ten times their chance; and yet Fox made rather a miserable business of life.

Nevertheless all these perversions of the doctrine of Jesus derived their moral force from his credit, and so had to keep his gospel alive. When the Protestants translated the Bible into the vernacular and let it loose among the people, they did an extremely dangerous thing, as the mischief which followed proves; but they incidentally let loose the sayings of Jesus in open competition with the sayings of Paul and Koheleth and David and Solomon and the authors of Job and the Pentateuch; and, as we have seen, Jesus seems to be the winning name. The glaring contradiction between his teaching and the practice of all the States and all the Churches is no longer hidden. And it may be that though nineteen centuries have passed since Jesus was born (the date of his birth is now quaintly given as 7 B.C., though some contend for 100 B.C.), and though his Church has not yet been founded nor his political system tried, the bankruptcy of all the other systems when audited by our vital statistics, which give us a final test for all political systems, is driving us hard into accepting him, not as a scapegoat, but as one who was much less of a fool in practical matters than we have hitherto all thought him.

THE ALTERNATIVE CHRISTS

Let us now clear up the situation a little. The New Testament tells two stories for two different sorts of readers. One is the old story of the achievement of our salvation by the sacrifice and atonement of a divine personage who was barbarously slain and rose again on the third day: the story as it was accepted by the apostles. And in this story the political, economic, and moral views of the Christ have no importance: the atonement is everything; and we are saved by our faith in it, and not by works or opinions (other than that particular opinion) bearing on practical affairs.

The other is the story of a prophet who, after expressing several very interesting opinions as to practical conduct, both personal and political, which are now of pressing importance, and instructing his disciples to carry them out in their daily life, lost his head; believed himself to be a crude legendary form of god; and under that delusion courted and suffered a cruel execution in the belief that he would rise from the dead and come in glory to reign over a regenerated world. In this form, the political, economic, and moral opinions of Jesus, as guides to conduct, are interesting and important: the rest is mere psychopathy and superstition. The accounts of the resurrection, the parthenogenetic birth, and the more incredible miracles are rejected as inventions; and such episodes as the conversation with the devil are classed with similar conversations recorded of St Dunstan, Luther, Bunyan, Swedenborg, and Blake.

CREDULITY NO CRITERION

This arbitrary acceptance and rejection of parts of the gospel is not peculiar to the Secularist view. We have seen Luke and

John reject Matthew's story of the massacre of the innocents and the flight into Egypt without ceremony. The notion that Matthew's manuscript is a literal and infallible record of facts, not subject to the errors that beset all earthly chroniclers, would have made John stare, being as it is a comparatively modern fancy of intellectually untrained people who keep the Bible on the same shelf with Napoleon's Book of Fate, Old Moore's Almanack, and handbooks of therapeutic herbalism. You may be a fanatical Salvationist and reject more miracle stories than Huxley did; and you may utterly repudiate Jesus as the Savior and yet cite him as a historical witness to the possession by men of the most marvellous thaumaturgical powers. "Christ Scientist" and Jesus the Mahatma are preached by people whom Peter would have struck dead as worse infidels than Simon Magus; and the Atonement is preached by Baptist and Congregationalist ministers whose views of the miracles are those of Ingersoll and Bradlaugh. Luther, who made a clean sweep of all the saints with their million miracles, and reduced the Blessed Virgin herself to the status of an idol, concentrated Salvationism to a point at which the most execrable murderer who believes in it when the rope is round his neck, flies straight to the arms of Jesus, whilst Tom Paine and Shelley fall into the bottomless pit to burn there to all eternity. And sceptical physicists like Sir William Crookes demonstrate by laboratory experiments that "mediums" like Dunglas Home can make the pointer of a spring-balance go round without touching the weight suspended from it.

Belief in Personal Immortality no Criterion

Nor is belief in individual immortality any criterion. Theosophists, rejecting vicarious atonement so sternly that they insist that the smallest of our sins brings its Karma, also insist on individual immortality and metempyschosis in order to provide an unlimited field for Karma to be worked out by the unredeemed sinner. The belief in the prolongation of individual life beyond

the grave is far more real and vivid among table-rapping Spiritualists than among conventional Christians. The notion that
those who reject the Christian (or any other) scheme of salvation
by atonement must reject also belief in personal immortality and
in miracles is as baseless as the notion that if a man is an atheist
he will steal your watch.

I could multiply these instances to weariness. The main difference that set Gladstone and Huxley by the ears is not one between
belief in supernatural persons or miraculous events and the
sternest view of such belief as a breach of intellectual integrity:
it is the difference between belief in the efficacy of the crucifixion
as an infallible cure for guilt, and a congenital incapacity for believing this, or (the same thing) desiring to believe it.

THE SECULAR VIEW NATURAL, NOT RATIONAL, THEREFORE INEVITABLE

It must therefore be taken as a flat fundamental modern fact,
whether we like it or not, that whilst many of us cannot believe
that Jesus got his curious grip of our souls by mere sentimentality,
neither can we believe that he was John Barleycorn. The more
our reason and study lead us to believe that Jesus was talking the
most penetrating good sense when he preached Communism;
when he declared that the reality behind the popular belief in God
was a creative spirit in ourselves called by him the Heavenly
Father and by us Evolution, Élan Vital, Life Force and other
names; when he protested against the claims of marriage and the
family to appropriate that high part of our energy that was meant
for the service of his Father, the more impossible it becomes for
us to believe that he was talking equally good sense when he so
suddenly announced that he was himself a visible concrete God;
that his flesh and blood were miraculous food for us; that he must
be tortured and slain in the traditional manner and would rise
from the dead after three days; and that at his Second Coming the
stars would fall from heaven and he become king of an earthly

paradise. But it is easy and reasonable to believe that an over-wrought preacher at last went mad as Swift and Ruskin and Nietzsche went mad. Every asylum has in it a patient suffering from the delusion that he is a god, yet otherwise sane enough. These patients do not nowadays declare that they will be barbarously slain and will rise from the dead, because they have lost that tradition of the destiny of godhead; but they claim everything appertaining to divinity that is within their knowledge.

Thus the gospels as memoirs and suggestive statements of sociological and biological doctrine, highly relevant to modern civilization, though ending in the history of a psychopathic delusion, are quite credible, intelligible, and interesting to modern thinkers. In any other light they are neither credible, intelligible, nor interesting except to people upon whom the delusion imposes.

"THE HIGHER CRITICISM"

Historical research and paleographic criticism will no doubt continue their demonstrations that the New Testament, like the Old, seldom tells a single story or expounds a single doctrine, and gives us often an accretion and conglomeration of widely discrete and even unrelated traditions and doctrines. But these disintegrations, though technically interesting to scholars, and gratifying or exasperating, as the case may be, to people who are merely defending or attacking the paper fortifications of the infallibility of the Bible, have hardly anything to do with the purpose of these pages. I have mentioned the fact that most of the authorities are now agreed (for the moment) that the date of the birth of Jesus may be placed at about 7 B.C.; but they do not therefore date their letters 1923, nor, I presume, do they expect me to do so. What I am engaged in is a criticism (in the Kantian sense) of an established body of belief which has become an actual part of the mental fabric of my readers; and I should be the most exasperating of triflers and pedants if I were to digress into a criticism of some other belief or nobelief which my readers might conceivably profess if they were erudite Scriptural paleographers and historians, in which case, by the way, they would have to change their views so frequently that the gospel they received in their childhood would dominate them after all by its superior persistency. The chaos of mere facts in which the Sermon on the Mount and the Ode to Charity suggest nothing but disputes as to whether they are interpolations or not, in which Jesus becomes nothing but a name suspected of belonging to ten different prophets or executed persons, in which Paul is only the man who could not possibly have written the epistles attributed to him, in which Chinese sages, Greek philosophers, Latin authors, and writers of ancient anonymous inscriptions are thrown at our heads as the sources of this or that scrap of the Bible, is neither a religion nor a criticism of religion: one does not offer the fact that a good deal of the medieval building in Peterborough Cathedral was found to be flagrant jerry-building as a criticism of the Dean's sermons. For good or evil, we have made a synthesis out of the literature we call the Bible; and though the discovery that there is a good deal of jerry-building in the Bible is interesting in its way, because everything about the Bible is interesting, it does not alter the synthesis very materially even for the paleographers, and does not alter it at all for those who know no more about modern paleography than Archbishop Ussher did. I have therefore indicated little more of the discoveries than Archbishop Ussher might have guessed for himself if he had read the Bible without prepossessions.

For the rest, I have taken the synthesis as it really lives and works in men. After all, a synthesis is what you want: it is the case you have to judge brought to an apprehensible issue for you. Even if you have little more respect for synthetic biography than for synthetic rubber, synthetic milk, and the still unachieved synthetic protoplasm which is to enable us to make different sorts of men as a pastrycook makes different sorts of tarts, the practical issue still lies as plainly before you as before the most credulous votaries of what pontificates as the Higher Criticism.

G

The Perils of Salvationism

The secular view of Jesus is powerfully reinforced by the increase in our day of the number of people who have had the means of educating and training themselves to the point at which they are not afraid to look facts in the face, even such terrifying facts as sin and death. The result is greater sternness in modern thought. The conviction is spreading that to encourage a man to believe that though his sins be as scarlet he can be made whiter than snow by an easy exercise of self-conceit, is to encourage him to be a rascal. It did not work so badly when you could also conscientiously assure him that if he let himself be caught napping in the matter of faith by death, a red-hot hell would roast him alive to all eternity. In those days a sudden death—the most enviable of all deaths—was regarded as the most frightful calamity. It was classed with plague, pestilence, and famine, battle and murder, in our prayers. But belief in that hell is fast vanishing. All the leaders of thought have lost it; and even for the rank and file it has fled to those parts of Ireland and Scotland which are still in the seventeenth century. Even there, it is tacitly reserved for the other fellow.

The Importance of Hell in the Salvation Scheme

The seriousness of throwing over hell whilst still clinging to the Atonement is obvious. If there is no punishment for sin there can be no self-forgiveness for it. If Christ paid our score, and if there is no hell and therefore no chance of our getting into trouble by forgetting the obligation, then we can be as wicked as we like with impunity inside the secular law, even from self-reproach, which becomes mere ingratitude to the Savior. On the other hand, if Christ did not pay our score, it still stands against us; and such debts make us extremely uncomfortable. The drive of evolution, which we call conscience and honor, seizes on such slips, and shames us to the dust for being so low in the scale as to be capable of them. The "saved" thief experiences an ecstatic happiness which can never come to the honest atheist: he is tempted to steal again to repeat the glorious sensation. But if the atheist steals he has no such happiness. He is a thief and knows that he is a thief. Nothing can rub that off him. He may try to soothe his shame by some sort of restitution or equivalent act of benevolence; but that does not alter the fact that he did steal; and his conscience will not be easy until he has conquered his will to steal and changed himself into an honest man by developing that divine spark within him which Jesus insisted on as the everyday reality of what the atheist denies.

Now though the state of the believers in the Atonement may thus be the happier, it is most certainly not more desirable from the point of view of the community. The fact that a believer is happier than a sceptic is no more to the point than the fact that a drunken man is happier than a sober one. The happiness of credulity is a cheap and dangerous quality of happiness, and by no means a necessity of life. Whether Socrates got as much happiness out of life as Wesley is an unanswerable question; but a nation of Socrateses would be much safer and happier than a nation of Wesleys; and its individuals would be higher in the evolutionary scale. At all events it is in the Socratic man and not in the Wesleyan that our hope lies now.

THE RIGHT TO REFUSE ATONEMENT

Consequently, even if it were mentally possible for all of us to believe in the Atonement, we should have to cry off it, as we evidently have a right to do. Every man to whom salvation is offered has an inalienable natural right to say "No, thank you: I prefer to retain my full moral responsibility: it is not good for me to be able to load a scapegoat with my sins: I should be less careful how I committed them if I knew they would cost me nothing." Then, too, there is the attitude of Ibsen: that iron moralist to whom the whole scheme of salvation was only an ignoble attempt to cheat God; to get into heaven without paying the price. To be let off, to beg for and accept eternal life as a present instead of earning it, would be mean enough even if we accepted the contempt of the Power on whose pity we were trading; but to bargain for a crown of glory as well! that was too much for Ibsen: it provoked him to exclaim, "Your God is an old man whom you cheat," and to lash the deadened conscience of the nineteenth century back to life with a whip of scorpions.

THE TEACHING OF CHRISTIANITY

And there I must leave the matter to such choice as your nature allows you. The honest teacher who has to make known to a novice the facts about Christianity cannot in any essential regard, I think, put the facts otherwise than as I have put them. If children are to be delivered from the proselytizing atheist on the one hand, and the proselytizing nun in the convent school on the other, with all the other proselytizers that lie between them, they must not be burdened with idle controversies as to whether there was ever such a person as Jesus or not. When Hume said that Joshua's campaigns were impossible, Whately did not wrangle about it: he proved, on the same lines, that the campaigns of Napoleon were impossible. Only fictitious characters will stand Hume's sort of examination: nothing will ever make Edward the Confessor and St Louis as real to us as Don Quixote and Mr Pickwick. We must cut the controversy short by declaring that there is the same evidence for the existence of Jesus as for that of any other person of his time; and the fact that you may not believe everything Matthew tells you no more disproves the existence of Jesus than the fact that you do not believe everything Macaulay tells you disproves the existence of William III. The gospel narratives in the main give you a biography which is quite credible and accountable on purely secular grounds when you have trimmed off everything that Hume or Grimm or Rousseau or Huxley or any modern bishop could reject as fanciful. Without going further than this, you can become a follower of Jesus just as you can become a follower of Confucius or Lao Tse, and may therefore call yourself a Jesuist, or even a Christian, if you hold, as the strictest Secularist quite legitimately may, that all prophets are inspired, and all men with a mission, Christs.

The teacher of Christianity has then to make known to the child, first the song of John Barleycorn, with the fields and seasons as witness to its eternal truth. Then, as the child's mind matures, it can learn, as historical and psychological phenomena, the tradition of the scapegoat, the Redeemer, the Atonement, the Resurrection, the Second Coming, and how, in a world saturated with this tradition, Jesus has been largely accepted as the long expected and often prophesied Redeemer, the Messiah, *the* Christ. It is open to the child also to accept him. If the child is built like Gladstone, he will accept Jesus as his Savior, and Peter and John the Baptist as the Savior's revealer and forerunner respectively. If he is built like Huxley, he will take the secular view, in spite of all that a pious family can do to prevent him. The important thing now is that the Gladstones and Huxleys should no longer waste their time irrelevantly and ridiculously wrangling about the Gadarene swine, and that they should make up their minds as to the soundness of the secular doctrines of Jesus; for it is about these that they may come to blows in our own time.

CHRISTIANITY AND THE EMPIRE

Finally, let us ask why it is that the old superstitions have so suddenly lost countenance that although, to the utter disgrace of the nation's leaders and rulers, the laws by which persecutors can destroy or gag all freedom of thought and speech in these matters are still unrepealed and ready to the hand of our bigots and fanatics (quite recently a respectable shopkeeper was convicted of "blasphemy" for saying that if a modern girl accounted for an illicit pregnancy by saying she had conceived of the Holy Ghost, we should know what to think: a remark which would never have occurred to him had he been properly taught how the story was grafted on the gospel), yet somehow they are used only against poor men, and that only in a half-hearted way. When we consider that from the time when the first scholar ventured to whisper as a professional secret that the Pentateuch could not possibly have been written by Moses to the time within my own recollection when Bishop Colenso, for saying the same thing openly, was inhibited from preaching and actually excommunicated, eight centuries elapsed (the point at issue, though technically interesting to paleographers and historians, having no more bearing on human welfare than the controversy as to whether uncial or cursive is the older form of writing); yet now, within fifty years of Colenso's heresy, there is not a Churchman of any authority living, or an educated layman, who could without ridicule declare that Moses wrote the Pentateuch as Pascal wrote his Thoughts or D'Aubigny his History of the Reformation, or that St Jerome wrote the passage about the three witnesses in the Vulgate, or that there are less than three different accounts of the creation jumbled together in the book of Genesis. Now the maddest Progressive will hardly contend that our growth in wisdom and liberality has been greater in the last half century than in the sixteen half centuries preceding: indeed it would be easier to sustain the thesis that the last fifty years have witnessed a distinct reaction from Victorian Liberalism to Collectivism which has perceptibly strengthened the State Churches. Yet the fact remains that whereas Byron's Cain, published a century ago, is a leading case on the point that there is no copyright in a blasphemous book, the Salvation Army might now include it among its publications without shocking anyone.

I suggest that the causes which have produced this sudden clearing of the air include the transformation of many modern States, notably the old self-contained French Republic and the tight little Island of Britain, into empires which overflow the frontiers of all the Churches. In India, for example, there are less than four million Christians out of a population of three hundred and sixteen and a half millions. The King of England is the defender of the faith; but what faith is now *the* faith? The inhabitants of this island would, within the memory of persons still living, have claimed that their faith is surely *the* faith of God, and that all others are heathen. But we islanders are only forty-five millions; and if we count ourselves all as Christians, there are still seventy-seven and a quarter million Mahometans in the Empire. Add to these the Hindoos and Buddhists, Sikhs and Jains, whom I was taught in my childhood, by way of religious instruction, to regard as gross idolaters consigned to eternal perdition, but whose faith I can now be punished for disparaging by a provocative word, and you have a total of over three hundred and forty-two and a quarter million heretics to swamp our forty-five million Britons, of whom, by the way, only six thousand call themselves distinctively "disciples of Christ," the rest being members of the Church of England and other denominations whose discipleship is less emphatically affirmed. In short, the Englishman of today, instead of being, like the forefathers whose ideas he clings to, a subject of a State practically wholly Christian, is now crowded, and indeed considerably overcrowded, into a corner of an Empire in which the Christians are a mere eleven per cent of the population; so that the Nonconformist who allows his umbrella stand to be sold up rather than pay rates towards the support of a Church of England school, finds himself paying taxes not only to endow the Church of Rome in Malta, but to send Christians to prison for the blasphemy of offering Bibles for sale in the streets of Khartoum.

Turn to France, a country ten times more insular in its preoccupation with its own language, its own history, its own character, than we, who have always been explorers and colonizers and grumblers. This once self-centred nation is forty millions strong. The total population of the French Republic is about one hundred and fourteen millions. The French are not in our hopeless Christian minority of eleven per cent; but they are in a minority of thirty-five per cent, which is fairly conclusive. And, being a more logical people than we, they have officially abandoned Christianity and declared that the French State has no specific religion.

Neither has the British State, though it does not say so. No doubt there are many innocent people in England who take Charlemagne's view, and would, as a matter of course, offer our eighty-nine per cent of "pagans, I regret to say" the alternative of death or Christianity but for a vague impression that these lost ones are all being converted gradually by the missionaries. But no statesman can entertain such ludicrously parochial delusions. No English king or French president can possibly govern on the assumption that the theology of Peter and Paul, Luther and Calvin, has any objective validity, or that the Christ is more than the Buddha, or Jehovah more than Krishna, or Jesus more or less human than Mahomet or Zoroaster or Confucius. He is actually compelled, in so far as he makes laws against blasphemy at all, to treat all the religions, including Christianity, as blasphemous when paraded before people who are not accustomed to them and do not want them. And even that is a concession to a mischievous intolerance which an empire should use its control of education to eradicate.

On the other hand, Governments cannot really divest themselves of religion, or even of dogma. When Jesus said that people should not only live but live more abundantly, he was dogmatizing; and many Pessimist sages, including Shakespear, whose hero begged his friend to refrain from suicide in the words "Absent thee from felicity awhile," would say dogmatizing very perniciously. Indeed many preachers and saints declare, some of them in the name of Jesus himself, that this world is a vale of tears, and that our lives had better be passed in sorrow and even in torment, as a preparation for a better life to come. Make these sad people comfortable; and they baffle you by putting on hair shirts.

None the less, Governments must proceed on dogmatic assumptions, whether they call them dogmas or not; and they must clearly be assumptions common enough to stamp those who reject them as eccentrics or lunatics. And the greater and more heterogeneous the population the commoner the assumptions must be. A Trappist monastery can be conducted on assumptions which would in twenty-four hours provoke the village at its gates to insurrection. That is because the monastery selects its people; and if a Trappist does not like it he can leave it. But a subject of the British Empire or the French Republic is not selected; and if he does not like it he must lump it; for emigration is practicable only within narrow limits, and seldom provides an effective remedy, all civilizations being now much alike.

To anyone capable of comprehending government at all it must be evident without argument that the set of fundamental assumptions drawn up in the thirty-nine articles or in the Westminster Confession are wildly impossible as political constitutions for modern empires. A personal profession of them by any person disposed to take such professions seriously would practically disqualify him for high imperial office. A Calvinist Viceroy of India and a Particular Baptist Secretary of State for Foreign Affairs would wreck the empire. The Stuarts wrecked even the tight little island which was the nucleus of the empire by their Scottish logic and theological dogma; and it may be sustained very plausibly that the alleged aptitude of the English for self-government, which is contradicted by every chapter of their history, is really only an incurable inaptitude for theology, and indeed for co-ordinated thought in any direction, which makes them equally impatient of systematic despotism and systematic good government: their history being that of a badly governed and accidentally free people (comparatively). Thus our success in colonizing, as far as it has not been produced by exterminating the natives, has been due to our indifference to the salvation of our subjects. Ireland is the exception which proves the rule; for Ireland, the standing instance of the inability of the English to colonize without extermination of natives, is also the one country under British rule in which the conquerors and colonizers proceeded on the assumption that their business was to establish

Protestantism as well as to make money and thereby secure at least the lives of the unfortunate inhabitants out of whose labor it could be made. At this moment Ulster is refusing to accept fellow-citizenship with the other Irish provinces because the south believes in St Peter and Bossuet, and the north in St Paul and Calvin. Imagine the effect of trying to govern India or Egypt from Belfast or from the Vatican!

The position is perhaps graver for France than for England, because the sixty-five per cent of French subjects who are neither French nor Christian nor Modernist includes some thirty millions of negroes who are susceptible, and indeed highly susceptible, of conversion to those salvationist forms of pseudo-Christianity which have produced all the persecutions and religious wars of the last fifteen hundred years. When the late explorer Sir Henry Stanley told me of the emotional grip which Christianity had over the Baganda tribes, and read me their letters, which were exactly like medieval letters in their literal faith and ever-present piety, I said "Can these men handle a rifle?" To which Stanley replied with some scorn "Of course they can, as well as any white man." Now at this moment (1915) a vast European war is being waged, in which the French are using Senegalese soldiers. I ask the French Government, which, like our own Government, is deliberately leaving the religious instruction of these negroes in the hands of missions of Petrine Catholics and Pauline Calvinists, whether they have considered the possibility of a new series of crusades, by ardent African Salvationists, to rescue Paris from the grip of the modern scientific "infidel," and to raise the cry of "Back to the Apostles: back to Charlemagne!"

We are more fortunate in that an overwhelming majority of our subjects are Hindoos, Mahometans, and Buddhists; that is, they have, as a prophylactic against salvationist Christianity, highly civilized religions of their own. Mahometanism, which Napoleon at the end of his career classed as perhaps the best popular religion for modern political use, might in some respects have arisen as a reformed Christianity if Mahomet had had to

deal with a population of seventeenth-century Christians instead
of Arabs who worshipped stones. As it is, men do not reject
Mahomet for Calvin; and to offer a Hindoo so crude a theology
as ours in exchange for his own, or our Jewish canonical literature
as an improvement on Hindoo scripture, is to offer old lamps for
older ones in a market where the oldest lamps, like old furniture
in England, are the most highly valued.

Yet, I repeat, government is impossible without a religion:
that is, without a body of common assumptions. The open mind
never acts: when we have done our utmost to arrive at a reasonable conclusion, we still, when we can reason and investigate no
more, must close our minds for the moment with a snap, and act
dogmatically on our conclusions. The man who waits to make an
entirely reasonable will dies intestate. A man so reasonable as to
have an open mind about theft and murder, or about the need for
food and reproduction, might just as well be a fool and a scoundrel for any use he could be as a legislator or a State official. The
modern pseudo-democratic statesman, who says that he is only
in power to carry out the will of the people, and moves only as
the cat jumps, is clearly a political and intellectual brigand. The
rule of the negative man who has no convictions means in practice
the rule of the positive mob. Freedom of conscience as Cromwell
used the phrase is an excellent thing; nevertheless if any man had
proposed to give effect to freedom of conscience as to cannibalism
in England, Cromwell would have laid him by the heels almost
as promptly as he would have laid a Roman Catholic, though in
Fiji at the same moment he would have supported heartily the
freedom of conscience of a vegetarian who disparaged the sacred
diet of Long Pig.

Here then comes in the importance of the repudiation by Jesus
of proselytism. His rule "Dont pull up the tares: sow the wheat:
if you try to pull up the tares you will pull up the wheat with it"
is the only possible rule for a statesman governing a modern empire, or a voter supporting such a statesman. There is nothing in
the teaching of Jesus that cannot be assented to by a Brahman, a

Mahometan, a Buddhist or a Jew, without any question of their conversion to Christianity. In some ways it is easier to reconcile a Mahometan to Jesus than a British parson, because the idea of a professional priest is unfamiliar and even monstrous to a Mahometan (the tourist who persists in asking who is the dean of St Sophia puzzles beyond words the sacristan who lends him a huge pair of slippers); and Jesus never suggested that his disciples should separate themselves from the laity: he picked them up by the wayside, where any man or woman might follow him. For priests he had not a civil word; and they shewed their sense of his hostility by getting him killed as soon as possible. He was, in short, a thorough-going anti-Clerical. And though, as we have seen, it is only by political means that his doctrine can be put into practice, he not only never suggested a sectarian theocracy as a form of government, and would certainly have prophesied the downfall of the late President Kruger if he had survived to his time, but, when challenged, he refused to teach his disciples not to pay tribute to Caesar, admitting that Caesar, who presumably had the kingdom of heaven within him as much as any disciple, had his place in the scheme of things. Indeed the apostles made this an excuse for carrying subservience to the State to a pitch of idolatry that ended in the theory of the divine right of kings, and provoked men to cut kings' heads off to restore some sense of proportion in the matter. Jesus certainly did not consider the overthrow of the Roman empire or the substitution of a new ecclesiastical organization for the Jewish Church or for the priesthood of the Roman gods as part of his program. He said that God was better than Mammon; but he never said that Tweedledum was better than Tweedledee; and that is why it is now possible for British citizens and statesmen to follow Jesus, though they cannot possibly follow either Tweedledum or Tweedledee without bringing the empire down with a crash on their heads. And at that I must leave it.

LONDON, *December* 1915

ANDROCLES AND THE LION
PROLOGUE

Overture: forest sounds, roaring of lions, Christian hymn faintly.
*A jungle path. A lion's roar, a melancholy suffering roar, comes
from the jungle. It is repeated nearer. The lion limps from the jungle
on three legs, holding up his right forepaw, in which a huge thorn
sticks. He sits down and contemplates it. He licks it. He shakes it.
He tries to extract it by scraping it along the ground, and hurts himself worse. He roars piteously. He licks it again. Tears drop from his
eyes. He limps painfully off the path and lies down under the trees,
exhausted with pain. Heaving a long sigh, like wind in a trombone,
he goes to sleep.*

*Androcles and his wife Megaera come along the path. He is a
small, thin, ridiculous little man who might be any age from thirty
to fifty-five. He has sandy hair, watery compassionate blue eyes,
sensitive nostrils, and a very presentable forehead; but his good points
go no further: his arms and legs and back, though wiry of their kind,
look shrivelled and starved. He carries a big bundle, is very poorly
clad, and seems tired and hungry.*

*His wife is a rather handsome pampered slattern, well fed and in
the prime of life. She has nothing to carry, and has a stout stick to
help her along.*

MEGAERA [*suddenly throwing down her stick*] I wont go another
step.

ANDROCLES [*pleading wearily*] Oh, not again, dear. Whats the
good of stopping every two miles and saying you wont go
another step? We must get on to the next village before night.
There are wild beasts in this wood: lions, they say.

MEGAERA. I dont believe a word of it. You are always threatening me with wild beasts to make me walk the very soul out of my
body when I can hardly drag one foot before another. We havnt
seen a single lion yet.

ANDROCLES. Well, dear, do you want to see one?

MEGAERA [*tearing the bundle from his back*] You cruel brute, you dont care how tired I am, or what becomes of me [*she throws the bundle on the ground*]: always thinking of yourself. Self! self! self! always yourself! [*She sits down on the bundle*].

ANDROCLES [*sitting down sadly on the ground with his elbows on his knees and his head in his hands*] We all have to think of ourselves occasionally, dear.

MEGAERA. A man ought to think of his wife sometimes.

ANDROCLES. He cant always help it, dear. You make me think of you a good deal. Not that I blame you.

MEGAERA. Blame me! I should think not indeed. Is it my fault that I'm married to you?

ANDROCLES. No, dear: that is my fault.

MEGAERA. Thats a nice thing to say to me. Arnt you happy with me?

ANDROCLES. I dont complain, my love.

MEGAERA. You ought to be ashamed of yourself.

ANDROCLES. I am, my dear.

MEGAERA. Youre not: you glory in it.

ANDROCLES. In what, darling?

MEGAERA. In everything. In making me a slave, and making yourself a laughing-stock. It's not fair. You get me the name of being a shrew with your meek ways, always talking as if butter wouldnt melt in your mouth. And just because I look a big strong woman, and because I'm goodhearted and a bit hasty, and because youre always driving me to do things I'm sorry for afterwards, people say "Poor man: what a life his wife leads him!" Oh, if they only knew! And you think I dont know. But I do, I do, [*screaming*] I do.

ANDROCLES. Yes, my dear: I know you do.

MEGAERA. Then why dont you treat me properly and be a good husband to me?

ANDROCLES. What can I do, my dear?

MEGAERA. What can you do! You can return to your duty, and

come back to your home and your friends, and sacrifice to the gods as all respectable people do, instead of having us hunted out of house and home for being dirty disreputable blaspheming atheists.

ANDROCLES. I'm not an atheist, dear: I am a Christian.

MEGAERA. Well, isnt that the same thing, only ten times worse? Everybody knows that the Christians are the very lowest of the low.

ANDROCLES. Just like us, dear.

MEGAERA. Speak for yourself. Dont you dare to compare me to common people. My father owned his own public-house; and sorrowful was the day for me when you first came drinking in our bar.

ANDROCLES. I confess I was addicted to it, dear. But I gave it up when I became a Christian.

MEGAERA. Youd much better have remained a drunkard. I can forgive a man being addicted to drink: it's only natural; and I dont deny I like a drop myself sometimes. What I cant stand is your being addicted to Christianity. And whats worse again, your being addicted to animals. How is any woman to keep her house clean when you bring in every stray cat and lost cur and lame duck in the whole countryside ? You took the bread out of my mouth to feed them: you know you did: dont attempt to deny it.

ANDROCLES. Only when they were hungry and you were getting too stout, dearie.

MEGAERA. Yes: insult me, do. [*Rising*] Oh! I wont bear it another moment. You used to sit and talk to those dumb brute beasts for hours, when you hadnt a word for me.

ANDROCLES. They never answered back, darling. [*He rises and again shoulders the bundle*].

MEGAERA. Well, if youre fonder of animals than of your own wife, you can live with them here in the jungle. Ive had enough of them and enough of you. I'm going back. I'm going home.

ANDROCLES [*barring the way back*] No, dearie: dont take on

like that. We cant go back. Weve sold everything: we should starve; and I should be sent to Rome and thrown to the lions—

MEGAERA. Serve you right! I wish the lions joy of you. [*Screaming*] Are you going to get out of my way and let me go home?

ANDROCLES. No, dear—

MEGAERA. Then I'll make my way through the forest; and when I'm eaten by the wild beasts youll know what a wife youve lost. [*She dashes into the jungle and nearly falls over the sleeping lion*]. Oh! Oh! Andy! Andy! [*She totters back and collapses into the arms of Androcles, who, crushed by her weight, falls on his bundle*].

ANDROCLES [*extracting himself from beneath her and slapping her hands in great anxiety*] What is it, my precious, my pet? Whats the matter? [*He raises her head. Speechless with terror, she points in the direction of the sleeping lion. He steals cautiously towards the spot indicated by Megaera. She rises with an effort and totters after him*].

MEGAERA. No, Andy: youll be killed. Come back.

The lion utters a long snoring sigh. Androcles sees the lion, and recoils fainting into the arms of Megaera, who falls back on the bundle. They roll apart and lie staring in terror at one another. The lion is heard groaning heavily in the jungle.

ANDROCLES [*whispering*] Did you see? A lion.

MEGAERA [*despairing*] The gods have sent him to punish us because youre a Christian. Take me away, Andy. Save me.

ANDROCLES [*rising*] Meggy: theres one chance for you. Itll take him pretty nigh twenty minutes to eat me (I'm rather stringy and tough) and you can escape in less time than that.

MEGAERA. Oh, dont talk about eating. [*The lion rises with a great groan and limps towards them*]. Oh! [*She faints*].

ANDROCLES [*quaking, but keeping between the lion and Megaera*] Dont you come near my wife, do you hear? [*The lion groans. Androcles can hardly stand for trembling*]. Meggy: run. Run for your life. If I take my eye off him, it's all up. [*The lion holds up his wounded paw and flaps it piteously before Androcles*]. Oh, he's lame, poor old chap! He's got a thorn in his paw. A frightfully big thorn. [*Full of sympathy*] Oh, poor old man! Did um get an awful thorn into um's tootsums wootsums? Has it made um too sick to eat a nice little Christian man for um's breakfast? Oh, a nice little Christian man will get um's thorn out for um; and then um shall eat the nice Christian man and the nice Christian man's nice big tender wifey pifey. [*The lion responds by moans of self-pity*]. Yes, yes, yes, yes, yes. Now, now [*taking the paw in his hand*], um is not to bite and not to scratch, not even if it hurts a very very little. Now make velvet paws. Thats right. [*He pulls gingerly at the thorn. The lion, with an angry yell of pain, jerks back his paw so abruptly that Androcles is thrown on his back*]. Steadeee! Oh, did the nasty cruel little Christian man hurt the sore paw? [*The lion moans assentingly but apologetically*]. Well, one more little pull and it will be all over. Just one little, little, leetle pull; and then um will live happily ever after. [*He gives the thorn another pull. The lion roars and snaps his jaws with a terrifying clash*]. Oh, mustnt frighten um's good kind doctor, um's affectionate nursey. That didnt hurt at all: not a bit. Just one more. Just to shew how the brave big lion can bear pain, not like the little crybaby Christian man. Oopsh! [*The thorn comes out. The lion yells with pain, and shakes his paw wildly*]. Thats it! [*Holding up the thorn*]. Now it's out. Now lick um's paw to take away the nasty inflammation. See? [*He licks his own hand. The lion nods intelligently and licks his paw industriously*]. Clever little liony-piony! Understands um's dear old friend Andy Wandy. [*The lion licks his face*]. Yes, kissums Andy Wandy. [*The lion wagging his tail violently, rises on his hind legs, and embraces Androcles, who makes a wry face and cries*] Velvet paws! Velvet paws! [*The lion draws in his claws*]. Thats right. [*He embraces the lion, who finally takes the end of his tail in one paw, places that tight round Androcles' waist, resting it on his hip. Androcles takes the other paw in his hand, stretches out his arm, and the two waltz rapturously round and round and finally away through the jungle*].

H

MEGAERA [*who has revived during the waltz*] Oh, you coward, you havnt danced with me for years; and now you go off dancing with a great brute beast that you havnt known for ten minutes and that wants to eat your own wife. Coward. Coward! Coward! [*She rushes off after them into the jungle*].

ACT I

Evening. The end of three converging roads to Rome. Three triumphal arches span them where they debouch on a square at the gate of the city. Looking north through the arches one can see the campagna threaded by the three long dusty tracks. On the east and west sides of the square are long stone benches. An old beggar sits on the east side, his bowl at his feet.

Through the eastern arch a squad of Roman soldiers tramps along escorting a batch of Christian prisoners of both sexes and all ages, among them one Lavinia, a good-looking resolute young woman, apparently of higher social standing than her fellow prisoners. A centurion, carrying his vinewood cudgel, trudges alongside the squad, on its right, in command of it. All are tired and dusty; but the soldiers are dogged and indifferent, the Christians lighthearted and determined to treat their hardships as a joke and encourage one another.

A bugle is heard far behind on the road, where the rest of the cohort is following.

CENTURION [*stopping*] Halt! Orders from the Captain. [*They halt and wait*]. Now then, you Christians, none of your larks. The captain's coming. Mind you behave yourselves. No singing. Look respectful. Look serious, if youre capable of it. See that big building over there! Thats the Coliseum. Thats where youll be thrown to the lions or set to fight the gladiators presently. Think of that; and itll help you to behave properly before the captain. [*The Captain arrives*]. Attention! Salute! [*The soldiers salute*].

A CHRISTIAN [*cheerfully*] God bless you, Captain!

THE CENTURION [*scandalized*] Silence!

The Captain, a patrician, handsome, about thirty-five, very cold and distinguished, very superior and authoritative, steps up on a stone seat at the west side of the square, behind the centurion, so as to dominate the others more effectually.

THE CAPTAIN. Centurion.

THE CENTURION [*standing at attention and saluting*] Sir?

THE CAPTAIN [*speaking stiffly and officially*] You will remind your men, Centurion, that we are now entering Rome. You will instruct them that once inside the gates of Rome they are in the presence of the Emperor. You will make them understand that the lax discipline of the march cannot be permitted here. You will instruct them to shave every day, not every week. You will impress on them particularly that there must be an end to the profanity and blasphemy of singing Christian hymns on the march. I have to reprimand you, Centurion, for not only allowing this, but actually doing it yourself.

THE CENTURION [*apologetic*] The men march better, Captain.

THE CAPTAIN. No doubt. For that reason an exception is made in the case of the march called Onward Christian Soldiers. This may be sung, except when marching through the forum or within hearing of the Emperor's palace; but the words must be altered to "Throw them to the Lions."

The Christians burst into shrieks of uncontrollable laughter, to the great scandal of the Centurion.

CENTURION. Silence! Silen-n-n-n-nce! Wheres your behavior? Is that the way to listen to an officer? [*To the Captain*] Thats what we have to put up with from these Christians every day, sir. Theyre always laughing and joking something scandalous. Theyve no religion: thats how it is.

LAVINIA. But I think the Captain meant us to laugh, Centurion. It was so funny.

CENTURION. Youll find out how funny it is when youre thrown to the lions tomorrow. [*To the Captain, who looks displeased*] Beg pardon, Sir. [*To the Christians*] Silennnnce!

THE CAPTAIN. You are to instruct your men that all intimacy with Christian prisoners must now cease. The men have fallen into habits of dependence upon the prisoners, especially the female prisoners, for cooking, repairs to uniforms, writing letters, and advice in their private affairs. In a Roman soldier such dependence is inadmissible. Let me see no more of it whilst we are in the city. Further, your orders are that in addressing Christian prisoners, the manners and tone of your men must express abhorrence and contempt. Any shortcoming in this respect will be regarded as a breach of discipline. [*He turns to the prisoners*] Prisoners.

CENTURION [*fiercely*] Prisonerrrrrs! Tention! Silence!

THE CAPTAIN. I call your attention, prisoners, to the fact that you may be called on to appear in the Imperial Circus at any time from tomorrow onwards according to the requirements of the managers. I may inform you that as there is a shortage of Christians just now, you may expect to be called on very soon.

LAVINIA. What will they do to us, Captain?

CENTURION. Silence!

THE CAPTAIN. The women will be conducted into the arena with the wild beasts of the Imperial Menagerie, and will suffer the consequences. The men, if of an age to bear arms, will be given weapons to defend themselves, if they choose, against the Imperial Gladiators.

LAVINIA. Captain: is there no hope that this cruel persecution—

CENTURION [*shocked*] Silence! Hold your tongue, there. Persecution, indeed!

THE CAPTAIN [*unmoved and somewhat sardonic*] Persecution is not a term applicable to the acts of the Emperor. The Emperor is the Defender of the Faith. In throwing you to the lions he will be upholding the interests of religion in Rome. If you were to throw him to the lions, that would no doubt be persecution.

The Christians again laugh heartily.

CENTURION [*horrified*] Silence, I tell you! Keep silence there. Did anyone ever hear the like of this?

LAVINIA. Captain: there will be nobody to appreciate your jokes when we are gone.

THE CAPTAIN [*unshaken in his official delivery*] I call the attention of the female prisoner Lavinia to the fact that as the Emperor is a divine personage, her imputation of cruelty is not only treason, but sacrilege. I point out to her further that there is no foundation for the charge, as the Emperor does not desire that any prisoner should suffer; nor can any Christian be harmed save through his or her own obstinacy. All that is necessary is to sacrifice to the gods: a simple and convenient ceremony effected by dropping a pinch of incense on the altar, after which the prisoner is at once set free. Under such circumstances you have only your own perverse folly to blame if you suffer. I suggest to you that if you cannot burn a morsel of incense as a matter of conviction, you might at least do so as a matter of good taste, to avoid shocking the religious convictions of your fellow citizens. I am aware that these considerations do not weigh with Christians; but it is my duty to call your attention to them in order that you may have no ground for complaining of your treatment, or of accusing the Emperor of cruelty when he is shewing you the most signal clemency. Looked at from this point of view, every Christian who has perished in the arena has really committed suicide.

LAVINIA. Captain: your jokes are too grim. Do you think it is easy for us to die. Our faith makes life far stronger and more wonderful in us than when we walked in darkness and had nothing to live for. Death is harder for us than for you: the martyr's agony is as bitter as his triumph is glorious.

THE CAPTAIN [*rather troubled, addressing her personally and gravely*] A martyr, Lavinia, is a fool. Your death will prove nothing.

LAVINIA. Then why kill me?

THE CAPTAIN. I mean that truth, if there be any truth, needs no martyrs.

LAVINIA. No; but my faith, like your sword, needs testing. Can you test your sword except by staking your life on it?

THE CAPTAIN [*suddenly resuming his official tone*] I call the attention of the female prisoner to the fact that Christians are not allowed to draw the Emperor's officers into arguments and put questions to them for which the military regulations provide no answer. [*The Christians titter*].

LAVINIA. Captain: how can you?

THE CAPTAIN. I call the female prisoner's attention specially to the fact that four comfortable homes have been offered her by officers of this regiment, of which she can have her choice the moment she chooses to sacrifice as all wellbred Roman ladies do. I have no more to say to the prisoners.

CENTURION. Dismiss! But stay where you are.

THE CAPTAIN. Centurion: you will remain here with your men in charge of the prisoners until the arrival of three Christian prisoners in the custody of a cohort of the tenth legion. Among these prisoners you will particularly identify an armorer named Ferrovius, of dangerous character and great personal strength, and a Greek tailor reputed to be a sorcerer, by name Androcles. You will add the three to your charge here and march them all to the Coliseum, where you will deliver them into the custody of the master of the gladiators and take his receipt, countersigned by the keeper of the beasts and the acting manager. You understand your instructions?

CENTURION. Yes, sir.

THE CAPTAIN. Dismiss. [*He throws off his air of parade, and descends from his perch. The Centurion seats himself on it and prepares for a nap, whilst his men stand at ease. The Christians sit down on the west side of the square, glad to rest. Lavinia alone remains standing to speak to the Captain*].

LAVINIA. Captain: is this man who is to join us the famous Ferrovius, who has made such wonderful conversions in the northern cities?

THE CAPTAIN. Yes. We are warned that he has the strength of an elephant and the temper of a mad bull. Also that he is stark mad. Not a model Christian, it would seem.

LAVINIA. You need not fear him if he is a Christian, Captain.

THE CAPTAIN [*coldly*] I shall not fear him in any case, Lavinia.

LAVINIA [*her eyes dancing*] How brave of you, Captain!

THE CAPTAIN. You are right: it was a silly thing to say. [*In a lower tone, humane and urgent*] Lavinia: do Christians know how to love?

LAVINIA [*composedly*] Yes, Captain: they love even their enemies.

THE CAPTAIN. Is that easy?

LAVINIA. Very easy, Captain, when their enemies are as handsome as you.

THE CAPTAIN. Lavinia: you are laughing at me.

LAVINIA. At you, Captain! Impossible.

THE CAPTAIN. Then you are flirting with me, which is worse. Dont be foolish.

LAVINIA. But such a very handsome captain.

THE CAPTAIN. Incorrigible! [*Urgently*] Listen to me. The men in that audience tomorrow will be the vilest of voluptuaries: men in whom the only passion excited by a beautiful woman is a lust to see her tortured and torn shrieking limb from limb. It is a crime to gratify that passion. It is offering yourself for violation by the whole rabble of the streets and the riff-raff of the court at the same time. Why will you not choose rather a kindly love and an honorable alliance?

LAVINIA. They cannot violate my soul. I alone can do that by sacrificing to false gods.

THE CAPTAIN. Sacrifice then to the true God. What does his name matter? We call him Jupiter. The Greeks call him Zeus. Call him what you will as you drop the incense on the altar flame: He will understand.

LAVINIA. No. I couldnt. That is the strange thing, Captain, that a little pinch of incense should make all that difference. Religion is such a great thing that when I meet really religious people we are friends at once, no matter what name we give to the divine will that made us and moves us. Oh, do you think that I, a woman, would quarrel with you for sacrificing to a woman god like Diana, if Diana meant to you what Christ means to me? No: we should kneel side by side before her altar like two children. But when men who believe neither in my god nor in their own—men who do not know the meaning of the word religion —when these men drag me to the foot of an iron statue that has become the symbol of the terror and darkness through which they walk, of their cruelty and greed, of their hatred of God and their oppression of man—when they ask me to pledge my soul before the people that this hideous idol is God, and that all this wickedness and falsehood is divine truth, I cannot do it, not if they could put a thousand cruel deaths on me. I tell you, it is physically impossible. Listen, Captain: did you ever try to catch a mouse in your hand? Once there was a dear little mouse that used to come out and play on my table as I was reading. I wanted to take him in my hand and caress him; and sometimes he got among my books so that he could not escape me when I stretched out my hand. And I did stretch out my hand; but it always came back in spite of me. I was not afraid of him in my heart; but my hand refused: it is not in the nature of my hand to touch a mouse. Well, Captain, if I took a pinch of incense in my hand and stretched it out over the altar fire, my hand would come back. My body would be true to my faith even if you could corrupt my mind. And all the time I should believe more in Diana than my perse-cutors have ever believed in anything. Can you understand that?

THE CAPTAIN [*simply*] Yes: I understand that. But my hand would not come back. The hand that holds the sword has been trained not to come back from anything but victory.

LAVINIA. Not even from death?

THE CAPTAIN. Least of all from death.

LAVINIA. Then I must not come back from death either. A woman has to be braver than a soldier.

THE CAPTAIN. Prouder, you mean.

LAVINIA [*startled*] Prouder! You call our courage pride!

THE CAPTAIN. There is no such thing as courage: there is only pride. You Christians are the proudest devils on earth.

LAVINIA [*hurt*] Pray God then my pride may never become a false pride. [*She turns away as if she did not wish to continue the conversation, but softens and says to him with a smile*] Thank you for trying to save me.

THE CAPTAIN. I knew it was no use; but one tries in spite of one's knowledge.

LAVINIA. Something stirs, even in the iron breast of a Roman soldier?

THE CAPTAIN. It will soon be iron again. I have seen many women die, and forgotten them in a week.

LAVINIA. Remember me for a fortnight, handsome Captain. I shall be watching you, perhaps.

THE CAPTAIN. From the skies? Do not deceive yourself, Lavinia. There is no future for you beyond the grave.

LAVINIA. What does that matter? Do you think I am only running away from the terrors of life into the comfort of heaven? If there were no future, or if the future were one of torment, I should have to go just the same. The hand of God is upon me.

THE CAPTAIN. Yes: when all is said, we are both patricians, Lavinia, and must die for our beliefs. Farewell. [*He offers her his hand. She takes it and presses it. He walks away, trim and calm. She looks after him for a moment, and cries a little as he disappears through the eastern arch. A trumpet-call is heard from the road through the western arch*].

CENTURION [*waking up and rising*] Cohort of the tenth with prisoners. Two file out with me to receive them. [*He goes out through the western arch, followed by four soldiers in two files*].

Lentulus and Metellus come into the square from the west side with a little retinue of servants. Both are young courtiers, dressed in the extremity of fashion. Lentulus is slender, fair-haired, epicene. Metellus is manly, compactly built, olive skinned, not a talker.

LENTULUS. Christians, by Jove! Lets chaff them.

METELLUS. Awful brutes. If you knew as much about them as I do you wouldnt want to chaff them. Leave them to the lions.

LENTULUS [*indicating Lavinia, who is still looking towards the arches after the Captain*] That woman's got a figure. [*He walks past her, staring at her invitingly; but she is preoccupied and is not conscious of him*]. Do you turn the other cheek when they kiss you?

LAVINIA [*starting*] What?

LENTULUS. Do you turn the other cheek when they kiss you, fascinating Christian?

LAVINIA. Dont be foolish. [*To Metellus, who has remained on her right, so that she is between them*] Please dont let your friend behave like a cad before the soldiers. How are they to respect and obey patricians if they see them behaving like street boys? [*Sharply to Lentulus*] Pull yourself together, man. Hold your head up. Keep the corners of your mouth firm; and treat me respectfully. What do you take me for?

LENTULUS [*irresolutely*] Look here, you know: I—you—I—

LAVINIA. Stuff! Go about your business. [*She turns decisively away and sits down with her comrades, leaving him disconcerted*].

METELLUS. You didnt get much out of that. I told you they were brutes.

LENTULUS. Plucky little filly! I suppose she thinks I care. [*With an air of indifference he strolls with Metellus to the east side of the square, where they stand watching the return of the Centurion through the western arch with his men, escorting three prisoners: Ferrovius, Androcles, and Spintho. Ferrovius is a powerful, choleric man in the prime of life, with large nostrils, staring eyes, and a thick neck: a man whose sensibilities are keen and violent to the verge of madness. Spintho is a debauchee, the wreck of a good-looking man gone hopelessly to the bad. Androcles is overwhelmed with grief, and is restraining his tears with great difficulty*].

THE CENTURION [*to Lavinia*] Here are some pals for you. This little bit is Ferrovius that you talk so much about. [*Ferrovius turns on him threateningly. The Centurion holds up his left forefinger in admonition*]. Now remember that youre a Christian, and that youve got to return good for evil. [*Ferrovius controls himself convulsively; moves away from temptation to the east side near Lentulus; clasps his hands in silent prayer; and throws himself on his knees*]. Thats the way to manage them, eh! This fine fellow [*indicating Androcles, who comes to his left, and makes Lavinia a heart-broken salutation*] is a sorcerer. A Greek tailor, he is. A real sorcerer, too: no mistake about it. The tenth marches with a leopard at the head of the column. He made a pet of the leopard; and now he's crying at being parted from it. [*Androcles sniffs lamentably*]. Aint you, old chap? Well, cheer up, we march with a Billy goat [*Androcles brightens up*] thats killed two leopards and ate a turkey-cock. You can have him for a pet if you like. [*Androcles, quite consoled, goes past the Centurion to Lavinia, and sits down contentedly on the ground on her left*]. This dirty dog [*collaring Spintho*] is a real Christian. He mobs the temples, he does [*at each accusation he gives the neck of Spintho's tunic a twist*]; he goes smashing things mad drunk, he does; he steals the gold vessels, he does; he assaults the priestesses, he does—yah! [*He flings Spintho into the middle of the group of prisoners*]. Youre the sort that makes duty a pleasure, you are.

SPINTHO [*gasping*] Thats it: strangle me. Kick me. Beat me. Revile me. Our Lord was beaten and reviled. Thats my way to heaven. Every martyr goes to heaven, no matter what he's done. That is so, isnt it, brother?

CENTURION. Well, if youre going to heaven, *I* dont want to go there. I wouldnt be seen with you.

LENTULUS. Haw! Good! [*Indicating the kneeling Ferrovius*]. Is this one of the turn-the-other-cheek gentlemen, Centurion?

CENTURION. Yes, sir. Lucky for you too, sir, if you want to take any liberties with him.

LENTULUS [*to Ferrovius*] You turn the other cheek when youre struck, I'm told.

FERROVIUS [*slowly turning his great eyes on him*] Yes, by the grace of God, I do, n o w.

LENTULUS. Not that youre a coward, of course; but out of pure piety.

FERROVIUS. I fear God more than man; at least I try to.

LENTULUS. Lets see. [*He strikes him on the cheek. Androcles makes a wild movement to rise and interfere; but Lavinia holds him down, watching Ferrovius intently. Ferrovius, without flinching, turns the other cheek. Lentulus, rather out of countenance, titters foolishly, and strikes him again feebly].* You know, I should feel ashamed if I let myself be struck like that, and took it lying down. But then I'm not a Christian: I'm a man. [*Ferrovius rises impressively and towers over him. Lentulus becomes white with terror; and a shade of green flickers in his cheek for a moment*].

FERROVIUS [*with the calm of a steam hammer*] I have not always been faithful. The first man who struck me as you have just struck me was a stronger man than you: he hit me harder than I expected. I was tempted and fell; and it was then that I first tasted bitter shame. I never had a happy moment after that until I had knelt and asked his forgiveness by his bedside in the hospital. [*Putting his hands on Lentulus's shoulders with paternal weight*]. But now I have learnt to resist with a strength that is not my own. I am not ashamed now, nor angry.

LENTULUS [*uneasily*] Er—good evening. [*He tries to move away*].

FERROVIUS [*gripping his shoulders*] Oh, do not harden your heart, young man. Come: try for yourself whether our way is not better than yours. I will now strike you on one cheek; and you will turn the other and learn how much better you will feel than if you gave way to the promptings of anger. [*He holds him with one hand and clenches the other fist*].

LENTULUS. Centurion: I call on you to protect me.

CENTURION. You asked for it, sir. It's no business of ours. Youve had two whacks at him. Better pay him a trifle and square it that way.

LENTULUS. Yes, of course. [*To Ferrovius*] It was only a bit of fun, I assure you: I meant no harm. Here. [*He proffers a gold coin*].

FERROVIUS [*taking it and throwing it to the old beggar, who snatches it up eagerly, and hobbles off to spend it*] Give all thou hast to the poor. Come, friend: courage! I may hurt your body for a moment; but your soul will rejoice in the victory of the spirit over the flesh. [*He prepares to strike*].

ANDROCLES. Easy, Ferrovius, easy: you broke the last man's jaw.

Lentulus, with a moan of terror, attempts to fly; but Ferrovius holds him ruthlessly.

FERROVIUS. Yes; but I saved his soul. What matters a broken jaw?

LENTULUS. Dont touch me, do you hear? The law—

FERROVIUS. The law will throw me to the lions tomorrow: what worse could it do were I to slay you? Pray for strength; and it shall be given to you.

LENTULUS. Let me go. Your religion forbids you to strike me.

FERROVIUS. On the contrary, it commands me to strike you. How can you turn the other cheek, if you are not first struck on the one cheek?

LENTULUS [*almost in tears*] But I'm convinced already that what you said is quite right. I apologize for striking you.

FERROVIUS [*greatly pleased*] My son: have I softened your heart? Has the good seed fallen in a fruitful place? Are your feet turning towards a better path?

LENTULUS [*abjectly*] Yes, yes. Theres a great deal in what you say.

FERROVIUS [*radiant*] Join us. Come to the lions. Come to suffering and death.

LENTULUS [*falling on his knees and bursting into tears*] Oh, help me. Mother! mother!

FERROVIUS. These tears will water your soul and make it bring forth good fruit, my son. God has greatly blessed my efforts at conversion. Shall I tell you a miracle—yes, a miracle—wrought by me in Cappadocia? A young man—just such a one as you, with golden hair like yours—scoffed at and struck me as you scoffed at and struck me. I sat up all night with that youth wrestling for his soul; and in the morning not only was he a Christian, but his hair was as white as snow. [*Lentulus falls in a dead faint*]. There, there: take him away. The spirit has over-wrought him, poor lad. Carry him gently to his house; and leave the rest to heaven.

CENTURION. Take him home. [*The servants, intimidated, hastily carry him out. Metellus is about to follow when Ferrovius lays his hand on his shoulder*].

FERROVIUS. You are his friend, young man. You will see that he is taken safely home.

METELLUS [*with awestruck civility*] Certainly, sir. I shall do whatever you think best. Most happy to have made your acquaintance, I'm sure. You may depend on me. Good evening, sir.

FERROVIUS [*with unction*] The blessing of heaven upon you and him.

Metellus follows Lentulus. The Centurion returns to his seat to resume his interrupted nap. The deepest awe has settled on the spectators. Ferrovius, with a long sigh of happiness, goes to Lavinia, and offers her his hand.

LAVINIA [*taking it*] So that is how you convert people, Ferrovius.

FERROVIUS. Yes: there has been a blessing on my work in spite of my unworthiness and my backslidings—all through my wicked, devilish temper. This man—

ANDROCLES [*hastily*] Dont slap me on the back, brother. She knows you mean me.

FERROVIUS. How I wish I were weak like our brother here! for then I should perhaps be meek and gentle like him. And yet there seems to be a special providence that makes my trials less than his. I hear tales of the crowd scoffing and casting stones and reviling the brethren; but when I come, all this stops: my influence calms the passions of the mob: they listen to me in silence; and infidels are often converted by a straight heart-to-heart talk with me. Every day I feel happier, more confident. Every day lightens the load of the great terror.

LAVINIA. The great terror? What is that?

Ferrovius shakes his head and does not answer. He sits down beside her on her left, and buries his face in his hands in gloomy meditation.

ANDROCLES. Well, you see, sister, he's never quite sure of himself. Suppose at the last moment in the arena, with the gladiators there to fight him, one of them was to say anything to annoy him, he might forget himself and lay that gladiator out.

LAVINIA. That would be splendid.

FERROVIUS [*springing up in horror*] What!

ANDROCLES. Oh, sister!

FERROVIUS. Splendid to betray my master, like Peter! Splendid to act like any common blackguard in the day of my proving! Woman: you are no Christian. [*He moves away from her to the middle of the square, as if her neighborhood contaminated him*].

LAVINIA [*laughing*] You know, Ferrovius, I am not always a Christian. I dont think anybody is. There are moments when I forget all about it, and something comes out quite naturally, as it did then.

SPINTHO. What does it matter? If you die in the arena, youll be a martyr; and all martyrs go to heaven, no matter what they have done. Thats so, isnt it, Ferrovius?

FERROVIUS. Yes: that is so, if we are faithful to the end.

LAVINIA. I'm not so sure.

SPINTHO. Dont say that. Thats blasphemy. Dont say that, I tell you. We shall be saved, no matter WHAT we do.

LAVINIA. Perhaps you men will all go into heaven bravely and in triumph, with your heads erect and golden trumpets sounding for you. But I am sure I shall only be allowed to squeeze myself in through a little crack in the gate after a great deal of begging. I am not good always: I have moments only.

SPINTHO. Youre talking nonsense, woman. I tell you, martyrdom pays all scores.

ANDROCLES. Well, let us hope so, brother, for your sake. Youve had a gay time, havnt you? with your raids on the temples. I cant help thinking that heaven will be very dull for a man of your temperament. [*Spintho snarls*]. Dont be angry: I say it only to console you in case you should die in your bed tonight in the natural way. Theres a lot of plague about.

SPINTHO [*rising and running about in abject terror*] I never thought of that. Oh Lord, spare me to be martyred. Oh, what a thought to put into the mind of a brother! Oh, let me be martyred today, now. I shall die in the night and go to hell. Youre a sorcerer: youve put death into my mind. Oh, curse you, curse you! [*He tries to seize Androcles by the throat*].

FERROVIUS [*holding him in a grasp of iron*] Whats this, brother? Anger! Violence! Raising your hand to a brother Christian!

SPINTHO. It's easy for you. Youre strong. Your nerves are all right. But I'm full of disease. [*Ferrovius takes his hand from him with instinctive disgust*]. Ive drunk all my nerves away. I shall have the horrors all night.

ANDROCLES [*sympathetic*] Oh, dont take on so, brother. We're all sinners.

SPINTHO [*snivelling, trying to feel consoled*] Yes: I daresay if the truth were known, youre all as bad as I am.

LAVINIA [*contemptuously*] Does that comfort you?

FERROVIUS [*sternly*] Pray, man, pray.

SPINTHO. Whats the good of praying? If we're martyred we shall go to heaven, shant we, whether we pray or not?

FERROVIUS. Whats that? Not pray! [*Seizing him again*] Pray this instant, you dog, you rotten hound, you slimy snake, you beastly goat, or—

SPINTHO. Yes: beat me: kick me. I forgive you: mind that.

FERROVIUS [*spurning him with loathing*] Yah! [*Spintho reels away and falls in front of Ferrovius*].

ANDROCLES [*reaching out and catching the skirt of Ferrovius's tunic*] Dear brother: if you wouldnt mind—just for my sake—

FERROVIUS. Well?

ANDROCLES. Dont call him by the names of the animals. Weve no right to. Ive had such friends in dogs. A pet snake is the best of company. I was nursed on goat's milk. Is it fair to them to call the like of him a dog or a snake or a goat?

I

FERROVIUS. I only meant that they have no souls.

ANDROCLES [*anxiously protesting*] Oh, believe me, they have. Just the same as you and me. I really dont think I could consent to go to heaven if I thought there were to be no animals there. Think of what they suffer here.

FERROVIUS. Thats true. Yes: that is just. They will have their share in heaven.

SPINTHO [*who has picked himself up and is sneaking past Ferrovius on his left, sneers derisively*]!!

FERROVIUS [*turning on him fiercely*] Whats that you say?

SPINTHO [*cowering*] Nothing.

FERROVIUS [*clenching his fist*] Do animals go to heaven or not?

SPINTHO. I never said they didnt.

FERROVIUS [*implacable*] Do they or do they not?

SPINTHO. They do: they do. [*Scrambling out of Ferrovius's reach*]. Oh, curse you for frightening me!

A bugle call is heard.

CENTURION [*waking up*] Tention! Form as before. Now then, prisoners: up with you and trot along spry. [*The soldiers fall in. The Christians rise*].

A man with an ox goad comes running through the central arch.

THE OX DRIVER. Here, you soldiers! clear out of the way for the Emperor.

THE CENTURION. Emperor! Where's the Emperor? You aint the Emperor, are you?

THE OX DRIVER. It's the menagerie service. My team of oxen is drawing the new lion to the Coliseum. You clear the road.

CENTURION. What! Go in after you in your dust, with half the town at the heels of you and your lion! Not likely. We go first.

THE OX DRIVER. The menagerie service is the Emperor's personal retinue. You clear out, I tell you.

CENTURION. You tell me, do you? Well, I'll tell you something. If the lion is menagerie service, the lion's dinner is menagerie service too. This [*pointing to the Christians*] is the lion's dinner. So back with you to your bullocks double quick;

and learn your place. March. [*The soldiers start*]. Now then, you Christians: step out there.

LAVINIA [*marching*] Come along, the rest of the dinner. I shall be the olives and anchovies.

ANOTHER CHRISTIAN [*laughing*] I shall be the soup.

ANOTHER. I shall be the fish.

ANOTHER. Ferrovius shall be the roast boar.

FERROVIUS [*heavily*] I see the joke. Yes, yes: I shall be the roast boar. Ha! ha! [*He laughs conscientiously and marches out with them*].

ANDROCLES [*following*] I shall be the mince pie. [*Each announcement is received with a louder laugh by all the rest as the joke catches on*].

CENTURION [*scandalized*] Silence! Have some sense of your situation. Is this the way for martyrs to behave? [*To Spintho, who is quaking and loitering*] I know what youll be at that dinner. Youll be the emetic. [*He shoves him rudely along*].

SPINTHO. It's too dreadful: I'm not fit to die.

CENTURION. Fitter than you are to live, you swine.

They pass from the square westward. The oxen, drawing a waggon with a great wooden cage and the lion in it, arrive through the central arch.

ACT II

Behind the Emperor's box at the Coliseum, where the performers assemble before entering the arena. In the middle a wide passage leading to the arena descends from the floor level under the imperial box. On both sides of this passage steps ascend to a landing at the back entrance to the box. The landing forms a bridge across the passage. At the entrance to the passage are two bronze mirrors, one on each side.

On the west side of this passage, on the right hand of anyone coming from the box and standing on the bridge, the martyrs are sitting on the steps. Lavinia is seated half-way up, thoughtful, trying to look death in the face. On her left Androcles consoles himself by nursing a cat. Ferrovius stands behind them, his eyes blazing, his figure stiff with intense resolution. At the foot of the steps crouches Spintho, with his head clutched in his hands, full of horror at the approach of martyrdom.

On the east side of the passage the gladiators are standing and sitting at ease, waiting, like the Christians, for their turn in the arena. One (Retiarius) is a nearly naked man with a net and a trident. Another (Secutor) is in armor with a sword. He carries a helmet with a barred visor. The editor of the gladiators sits on a chair a little apart from them.

The Call Boy enters from the passage.

THE CALL BOY. Number six. Retiarius versus Secutor.

The gladiator with the net picks it up. The gladiator with the helmet puts it on; and the two go into the arena, the net thrower taking out a little brush and arranging his hair as he goes, the other tightening his straps and shaking his shoulders loose. Both look at themselves in the mirrors before they enter the passage.

LAVINIA. Will they really kill one another?

SPINTHO. Yes, if the people turn down their thumbs.

THE EDITOR. You know nothing about it. The people indeed! Do you suppose we would kill a man worth perhaps fifty talents to please the riffraff? I should like to catch any of my men at it.

SPINTHO. I thought—

THE EDITOR [contemptuously] You thought! Who cares what you think? Youll be killed all right enough.

SPINTHO [groans and again hides his face]!!!

LAVINIA. Then is nobody ever killed except us poor Christians?

THE EDITOR. If the vestal virgins turn down their thumbs, thats another matter. Theyre ladies of rank.

LAVINIA. Does the Emperor ever interfere?

THE EDITOR. Oh, yes: he turns his thumb up fast enough if the vestal virgins want to have one of his pet fighting men killed.

ANDROCLES. But dont they ever just only pretend to kill one another? Why shouldnt you pretend to die, and get dragged out as if you were dead; and then get up and go home, like an actor?

THE EDITOR. See here: you want to know too much. There will be no pretending about the new lion: let that be enough for you. He's hungry.

SPINTHO [groaning with horror] Oh, Lord! cant you stop talking about it? Isnt it bad enough for us without that?

ANDROCLES. I'm glad he's hungry. Not that I want him to suffer, poor chap! but then he'll enjoy eating me so much more. Theres a cheerful side to everything.

THE EDITOR [rising and striding over to Androcles] Here: dont you be obstinate. Come with me and drop the pinch of incense on the altar. Thats all you need do to be let off.

ANDROCLES. No: thank you very much indeed; but I really mustnt.

THE EDITOR. What! Not to save your life?

ANDROCLES. I'd rather not. I couldnt sacrifice to Diana: she's a huntress, you know, and kills things.

THE EDITOR. That dont matter. You can choose your own altar. Sacrifice to Jupiter: he likes animals: he turns himself into an animal when he goes off duty.

ANDROCLES. No: it's very kind of you; but I feel I cant save myself that way.

THE EDITOR. But I dont ask you to do it to save yourself: I ask you to do it to oblige me personally.

ANDROCLES [*scrambling up in the greatest agitation*] Oh, please dont say that. This is dreadful. You mean so kindly by me that it seems quite horrible to disoblige you. If you could arrange for me to sacrifice when theres nobody looking, I shouldnt mind. But I must go into the arena with the rest. My honor, you know.

THE EDITOR. Honor! The honor of a tailor?

ANDROCLES [*apologetically*] Well, perhaps honor is too strong an expression. Still, you know, I couldnt allow the tailors to get a bad name through me.

THE EDITOR. How much will you remember of all that when you smell the beast's breath and see his jaws opening to tear out your throat?

SPINTHO [*rising with a yell of terror*] I cant bear it. Wheres the altar? I'll sacrifice.

FERROVIUS. Dog of an apostate. Iscariot!

SPINTHO. I'll repent afterwards. I fully mean to die in the arena: I'll die a martyr and go to heaven; but not this time, not now, not until my nerves are better. Besides, I'm too young: I want to have just one more good time. [*The gladiators laugh at him*]. Oh, will no one tell me where the altar is? [*He dashes into the passage and vanishes*].

ANDROCLES [*to the Editor, pointing after Spintho*] Brother: I cant do that, not even to oblige you. Dont ask me.

THE EDITOR. Well, if youre determined to die, I cant help you. But I wouldnt be put off by a swine like that.

FERROVIUS. Peace, peace: tempt him not. Get thee behind him, Satan.

THE EDITOR [*flushing with rage*] For two pins I'd take a turn in the arena myself today, and pay you out for daring to talk to me like that.

Ferrovius springs forward.

LAVINIA [*rising quickly and interposing*] Brother, brother: you forget.

FERROVIUS [*curbing himself by a mighty effort*] Oh, my temper, my wicked temper! [*To the Editor, as Lavinia sits down again, reassured*] Forgive me, brother. My heart was full of wrath: I should have been thinking of your dear precious soul.

THE EDITOR. Yah! [*He turns his back on Ferrovius contemptuously, and goes back to his seat*].

FERROVIUS [*continuing*] And I forgot it all: I thought of nothing but offering to fight you with one hand tied behind me.

THE EDITOR [*turning pugnaciously*] What!

FERROVIUS [*on the border line between zeal and ferocity*] Oh, dont give way to pride and wrath, brother. I could do it so easily. I could—

They are separated by the Menagerie Keeper, who rushes in from the passage, furious.

THE KEEPER. Heres a nice business! Who let that Christian out of here down to the dens when we were changing the lion into the cage next the arena?

THE EDITOR. Nobody let him. He let himself.

THE KEEPER. Well, the lion's ate him.

Consternation. The Christians rise, greatly agitated. The gladiators sit callously, but are highly amused. All speak or cry out or laugh at once. Tumult.

LAVINIA. Oh, poor wretch! FERROVIUS. The apostate has perished. Praise be to God's justice! ANDROCLES. The poor beast was starving. It couldnt help itself. THE CHRISTIANS. What! Ate him! How frightful! How terrible! Without a moment to repent! God be merciful to him, a sinner! Oh, I cant bear to think of it! In the midst of his sin! Horrible, horrible! THE EDITOR. Serve the rotter right! THE GLADIATORS. Just walked into it, he did. He's martyred all right enough. Good old lion! Old Jock doesn't like that: look at his face. Devil a better! The Emperor will laugh when he hears of it. I cant help smiling. Ha ha ha!!!!!

THE KEEPER. Now his appetite's taken off, he wont as much as look at another Christian for a week.

ANDROCLES. Couldnt you have saved him, brother?

THE KEEPER. Saved him! Saved him from a lion that I'd just got mad with hunger! a wild one that came out of the forest not four weeks ago! He bolted him before you could say Balbus.

LAVINIA [*sitting down again*] Poor Spintho! And it wont even count as martyrdom!

THE KEEPER. Serve him right! What call had he to walk down the throat of one of my lions before he was asked?

ANDROCLES. Perhaps the lion wont eat me now.

THE KEEPER. Yes: thats just like a Christian: think only of yourself! What am *I* to do? What am I to say to the Emperor when he sees one of my lions coming into the arena half asleep?

THE EDITOR. Say nothing. Give your old lion some bitters and a morsel of fried fish to wake up his appetite. [*Laughter*].

THE KEEPER. Yes: it's easy for you to talk; but—

THE EDITOR [*scrambling to his feet*] Sh! Attention there! The Emperor. [*The Keeper bolts precipitately into the passage. The gladiators rise smartly and form into line*].

The Emperor enters on the Christians' side, conversing with Metellus, and followed by his suite.

THE GLADIATORS. Hail, Caesar! those about to die salute thee.

CAESAR. Good morrow, friends.

Metellus shakes hands with the Editor, who accepts his condescension with bluff respect.

LAVINIA. Blessing, Caesar, and forgiveness!

CAESAR [*turning in some surprise at the salutation*] There is no forgiveness for Christianity.

LAVINIA. I did not mean that, Caesar. I mean that we forgive you.

METELLUS. An inconceivable liberty! Do you not know, woman, that the Emperor can do no wrong and therefore cannot be forgiven?

LAVINIA. I expect the Emperor knows better. Anyhow, we forgive him.

THE CHRISTIANS. Amen!

CAESAR. Metellus: you see now the disadvantage of too much

severity. These people have no hope; therefore they have nothing to restrain them from saying what they like to me. They are almost as impertinent as the gladiators. Which is the Greek sorcerer?

ANDROCLES [*humbly touching his forelock*] Me, your Worship.

CAESAR. My Worship! Good! A new title. Well: what miracles can you perform?

ANDROCLES. I can cure warts by rubbing them with my tailor's chalk; and I can live with my wife without beating her.

CAESAR. Is that all?

ANDROCLES. You dont know her, Caesar, or you wouldnt say that.

CAESAR. Ah, well, my friend, we shall no doubt contrive a happy release for you. Which is Ferrovius?

FERROVIUS. I am he.

CAESAR. They tell me you can fight.

FERROVIUS. It is easy to fight. *I* can die, Caesar.

CAESAR. That is still easier, is it not?

FERROVIUS. Not to me, Caesar. Death comes hard to my flesh; and fighting comes very easily to my spirit [*beating his breast and lamenting*] Oh, sinner that I am! [*He throws himself down on the steps, deeply discouraged*].

CAESAR. Metellus: I should like to have this man in the Pretorian Guard.

METELLUS. *I* should not, Caesar. He looks a spoilsport. There are men in whose presence it is impossible to have any fun: men who are a sort of walking conscience. He would make us all uncomfortable.

CAESAR. For that reason, perhaps, it might be as well to have him. An Emperor can hardly have too many consciences. [*To Ferrovius*] Listen, Ferrovius. [*Ferrovius shakes his head and will not look up*]. You and your friends shall not be outnumbered today in the arena. You shall have arms; and there will be no more than one gladiator to each Christian. If you come out of the arena alive, I will consider favorably any request of yours, and give you a place in the Pretorian Guard. Even if the request be that no questions be asked about your faith I shall perhaps not refuse it.

FERROVIUS. I will not fight. I will die. Better stand with the archangels than with the Pretorian Guard.

CAESAR. I cannot believe that the archangels—whoever they may be—would not prefer to be recruited from the Pretorian Guard. However, as you please. Come: let us see the show.

As the Court ascends the steps, Secutor and Retiarius return from the arena through the passage: Secutor covered with dust and very angry: Retiarius grinning.

SECUTOR. Ha, the Emperor. Now we shall see. Caesar: I ask you whether it is fair for the Retiarius, instead of making a fair throw of his net at me, to swish it along the ground and throw the dust in my eyes, and then catch me when I'm blinded. If the vestals had not turned up their thumbs I should have been a dead man.

CAESAR [*halting on the stair*] There is nothing in the rules against it.

SECUTOR [*indignantly*] Caesar: is it a dirty trick or is it not?

CAESAR. It is a dusty one, my friend. [*Obsequious laughter*]. Be on your guard next time.

SECUTOR. Let him be on his guard. Next time I'll throw my sword at his heels and strangle him with his own net before he can hop off. [*To the Retiarius*] You see if I dont. [*He goes out past the gladiators, sulky and furious*].

CAESAR [*to the chuckling Retiarius*] These tricks are not wise, my friend. The audience likes to see a dead man in all his beauty and splendor. If you smudge his face and spoil his armor they will shew their displeasure by not letting you kill him. And when your turn comes, they will remember it against you and turn their thumbs down.

THE RETIARIUS. Perhaps that is why I did it, Caesar. He bet me ten sesterces that he would vanquish me. If I had had to kill him I should not have had the money.

CAESAR [*indulgent, laughing*] You rogues: there is no end to your tricks. I'll dismiss you all and have elephants to fight. They fight fairly. [*He goes up to his box, and knocks at it. It is opened from within by the Captain, who stands as on parade to let him pass*].

The Call Boy comes from the passage, followed by three attendants carrying respectively a bundle of swords, some helmets, and some breastplates and pieces of armor which they throw down in a heap.

THE CALL BOY. By your leave, Caesar. Number eleven! Gladiators and Christians!

Ferrovius springs up, ready for martyrdom. The other Christians take the summons as best they can, some joyful and brave, some patient and dignified, some tearful and helpless, some embracing one another with emotion. The Call Boy goes back into the passage.

CAESAR [*turning at the door of the box*] The hour has come, Ferrovius. I shall go into my box and see you killed, since you scorn the Pretorian Guard. [*He goes into the box. The Captain shuts the door, remaining inside with the Emperor, Metellus and the rest of the suite disperse to their seats. The Christians, led by Ferrovius, move towards the passage*].

LAVINIA [*to Ferrovius*] Farewell.

THE EDITOR. Steady there. You Christians have got to fight. Here! arm yourselves.

FERROVIUS [*picking up a sword*] I'll die sword in hand to shew people that I could fight if it were my Master's will, and that I could kill the man who kills me if I chose.

THE EDITOR. Put on that armor.

FERROVIUS. No armor.

THE EDITOR [*bullying him*] Do what youre told. Put on that armor.

FERROVIUS [*gripping the sword and looking dangerous*] I said, No armor.

THE EDITOR. And what am I to say when I am accused of sending a naked man in to fight my men in armor?

FERROVIUS. Say your prayers, brother; and have no fear of the princes of this world.

THE EDITOR. Tsha! You obstinate fool! [*He bites his lips irresolutely, not knowing exactly what to do*].

ANDROCLES [*to Ferrovius*] Farewell, brother, till we meet in the sweet by-and-by.

THE EDITOR [*to Androcles*] You are going too. Take a sword there; and put on any armor you can find to fit you.

ANDROCLES. No, really: I cant fight: I never could: I cant bring myself to dislike anyone enough. I'm to be thrown to the lions with the lady.

THE EDITOR. Then get out of the way and hold your noise. [*Androcles steps aside with cheerful docility*]. Now then! Are you all ready there?

A trumpet is heard from the arena.

FERROVIUS [*starting convulsively*] Heaven give me strength!

THE EDITOR. Aha! That frightens you, does it?

FERROVIUS. Man: there is no terror like the terror of that sound to me. When I hear a trumpet or a drum or the clash of steel or the hum of the catapult as the great stone flies, fire runs through my veins: I feel my blood surge up hot behind my eyes: I must charge: I must strike: I must conquer: Caesar himself will not be safe in his imperial seat if once that spirit gets loose in me. Oh, brothers, pray! exhort me! remind me that if I raise my sword my honor falls and my Master is crucified afresh.

ANDROCLES. Just keep thinking how cruelly you might hurt the poor gladiators.

FERROVIUS. It does not hurt a man to kill him.

LAVINIA. Nothing but faith can save you.

FERROVIUS. Faith! Which faith? There are two faiths. There is our faith. And there is the warrior's faith, the faith in fighting, the faith that sees God in the sword. How if that faith should overwhelm me?

LAVINIA. You will find your real faith in the hour of trial.

FERROVIUS. That is what I fear. I know that I am a fighter. How can I feel sure that I am a Christian?

ANDROCLES. Throw away the sword, brother.

FERROVIUS. I cannot. It cleaves to my hand. I could as easily throw a woman I loved from my arms. [*Starting*] Who spoke that blasphemy? Not I.

LAVINIA. I cant help you, friend. I cant tell you not to save your own life. Something wilful in me wants to see you fight your way into heaven.

FERROVIUS. Ha!

ANDROCLES. But if you are going to give up our faith, brother, why not do it without hurting anybody? Dont fight them. Burn the incense.

FERROVIUS. Burn the incense! Never.

LAVINIA. That is only pride, Ferrovius.

FERROVIUS. Only pride! What is nobler than pride? [*Conscience stricken*] Oh, I'm steeped in sin. I'm proud of my pride.

LAVINIA. They say we Christians are the proudest devils on earth—that only the weak are meek. Oh, I am worse than you. I ought to send you to death; and I am tempting you.

ANDROCLES. Brother, brother: let them rage and kill: let us be brave and suffer. You must go as a lamb to the slaughter.

FERROVIUS. Aye, aye: that is right. Not as a lamb is slain by the butcher; but as a butcher might let himself be slain by a [*looking at the Editor*] by a silly ram whose head he could fetch off in one twist.

Before the Editor can retort, the Call Boy rushes up through the passage, and the Captain comes from the Emperor's box and descends the steps.

THE CALL BOY. In with you: into the arena. The stage is waiting.

THE CAPTAIN. The Emperor is waiting. [*To the Editor*] What are you dreaming of, man? Send your men in at once.

THE EDITOR. Yes, sir: it's these Christians hanging back.

FERROVIUS [*in a voice of thunder*] Liar!

THE EDITOR [*not heeding him*] March. [*The gladiators told off to fight with the Christians march down the passage*] Follow up there, you.

THE CHRISTIAN MEN AND WOMEN [*as they part*] Be steadfast,

brother. Farewell. Hold up the faith, brother. Farewell. Go to glory, dearest. Farewell. Remember: we are praying for you. Farewell. Be strong, brother. Farewell. Dont forget that the divine love and our love surround you. Farewell. Nothing can hurt you: remember that, brother. Farewell. Eternal glory, dearest. Farewell.

THE EDITOR [*out of patience*] Shove them in, there.

The remaining gladiators and the Call Boy make a movement towards them.

FERROVIUS [*interposing*] Touch them, dogs; and we die here, and cheat the heathen of their spectacle. [*To his fellow Christians*] Brothers: the great moment has come. That passage is your hill to Calvary. Mount it bravely, but meekly; and remember! not a word of reproach, not a blow nor a struggle. Go. [*They go out through the passage. He turns to Lavinia*] Farewell.

LAVINIA. You forget: I must follow before you are cold.

FERROVIUS. It is true. Do not envy me because I pass before you to glory. [*He goes through the passage*].

THE EDITOR [*to the Call Boy*] Sickening work, this. Why cant they all be thrown to the lions? It's not a man's job. [*He throws himself moodily into his chair*].

The remaining gladiators go back to their former places indifferently. The Call Boy shrugs his shoulders and squats down at the entrance to the passage, near the Editor.

Lavinia and the Christian women sit down again, wrung with grief, some weeping silently, some praying, some calm and steadfast. Androcles sits down at Lavinia's feet. The Captain stands on the stairs, watching her curiously.

ANDROCLES. I'm glad I havnt to fight. That would really be an awful martyrdom. I am lucky.

LAVINIA [*looking at him with a pang of remorse*] Androcles: burn the incense: youll be forgiven. Let my death atone for both. I feel as if I were killing you.

ANDROCLES. Dont think of me, sister. Think of yourself. That will keep your heart up.

The Captain laughs sardonically.

LAVINIA [*startled: she had forgotten his presence*] Are you there, handsome Captain? Have you come to see me die?

THE CAPTAIN [*coming to her side*] I am on duty with the Emperor, Lavinia.

LAVINIA. Is it part of your duty to laugh at us?

THE CAPTAIN. No: that is part of my private pleasure. Your friend here is a humorist. I laughed at his telling you to think of yourself to keep up your heart. *I* say, think of yourself and burn the incense.

LAVINIA. He is not a humorist: he was right. You ought to know that, Captain: you have been face to face with death.

THE CAPTAIN. Not with certain death, Lavinia. Only death in battle, which spares more men than death in bed. What you are facing is certain death. You have nothing left now but your faith in this craze of yours: this Christianity. Are your Christian fairy stories any truer than our stories about Jupiter and Diana, in which, I may tell you, I believe no more than the Emperor does, or any educated man in Rome?

LAVINIA. Captain: all that seems nothing to me now. I'll not say that death is a terrible thing; but I will say that it is so real a thing that when it comes close, all the imaginary things—all the stories, as you call them—fade into mere dreams beside that inexorable reality. I know now that I am not dying for stories or dreams. Did you hear of the dreadful thing that happened here while we were waiting?

THE CAPTAIN. I heard that one of your fellows bolted, and ran right into the jaws of the lion. I laughed. I still laugh.

LAVINIA. Then you dont understand what that meant?

THE CAPTAIN. It meant that the lion had a cur for his breakfast.

LAVINIA. It meant more than that, Captain. It meant that a man cannot die for a story and a dream. None of us believed the stories and the dreams more devoutly than poor Spintho; but he could not face the great reality. What he would have called my faith has been oozing away minute by minute whilst Ive been sitting here, with death coming nearer and nearer, with reality becoming realer and realer, with stories and dreams fading away into nothing.

THE CAPTAIN. Are you then going to die for nothing?

LAVINIA. Yes: that is the wonderful thing. It is since all the stories and dreams have gone that I have now no doubt at all that I must die for something greater than dreams or stories.

THE CAPTAIN. But for what?

LAVINIA. I dont know. If it were for anything small enough to know, it would be too small to die for. I think I'm going to die for God. Nothing else is real enough to die for.

THE CAPTAIN. What is God?

LAVINIA. When we know that, Captain, we shall be gods ourselves.

THE CAPTAIN. Lavinia: come down to earth. Burn the incense and marry me.

LAVINIA. Handsome Captain: would you marry me if I hauled down the flag in the day of battle and burnt the incense? Sons take after their mothers, you know. Do you want your son to be a coward?

THE CAPTAIN [*strongly moved*] By great Diana, I think I would strangle you if you gave in now.

LAVINIA [*putting her hand on the head of Androcles*] The hand of God is on us three, Captain.

THE CAPTAIN. What nonsense it all is! And what a monstrous thing that you should die for such nonsense, and that I should look on helplessly when my whole soul cries out against it! Die then if you must; but at least I can cut the Emperor's throat and then my own when I see your blood.

The Emperor throws open the door of his box angrily, and appears in wrath on the threshold. The Editor, the Call Boy, and the gladiators spring to their feet.

THE EMPEROR. The Christians will not fight, and your curs cannot get their blood up to attack them. It's all that fellow with the blazing eyes. Send for the whip. [*The Call Boy rushes out on the east side for the whip*]. If that will not move them, bring the hot irons. The man is like a mountain. [*He returns angrily into the box and slams the door*].

The Call Boy returns with a man in a hideous Etruscan mask, carrying a whip. They both rush down the passage into the arena.

LAVINIA [*rising*] Oh, that is unworthy. Can they not kill him without dishonoring him?

ANDROCLES [*scrambling to his feet and running into the middle of the space between the staircases*] It's dreadful. Now *I* want to fight. I cant bear the sight of a whip. The only time I ever hit a man was when he lashed an old horse with a whip. It was terrible: I danced on his face when he was on the ground. He mustnt strike Ferrovius: I'll go into the arena and kill him first. [*He makes a wild dash into the passage. As he does so a great clamor is heard from the arena, ending in wild applause. The gladiators listen and look inquiringly at one another*].

THE EDITOR. Whats up now?

LAVINIA [*to the Captain*] What has happened, do you think?

THE CAPTAIN. What can happen? They are killing them, I suppose.

ANDROCLES [*running in through the passage, screaming with horror and hiding his eyes*]!!!

LAVINIA. Androcles, Androcles: whats the matter?

ANDROCLES. Oh dont ask me, dont ask me. Something too dreadful. Oh! [*He crouches by her and hides his face in her robe, sobbing*].

THE CALL BOY [*rushing through from the passage as before*] Ropes and hooks there! Ropes and hooks!

THE EDITOR. Well, need you excite yourself about it? [*Another burst of applause*].

Two slaves in Etruscan masks, with ropes and drag hooks, hurry in.

ONE OF THE SLAVES. How many dead?

THE CALL BOY. Six. [*The slave blows a whistle twice; and four more masked slaves rush through into the arena with the same*

K

apparatus]. And the basket. Bring the baskets. [*The slave whistles three times, and runs through the passage with his companion*].

THE CAPTAIN. Who are the baskets for?

THE CALL BOY. For the whip. He's in pieces. Theyre all in pieces, more or less. [*Lavinia hides her face*].

Two more masked slaves come in with a basket and follow the others into the arena, as the Call Boy turns to the gladiators and exclaims, exhausted, Boys: he's killed the lot.

THE EMPEROR [*again bursting from his box, this time in an ecstasy of delight*] Where is he? Magnificent! He shall have a laurel crown.

Ferrovius, madly waving his bloodstained sword, rushes through the passage in despair, followed by his co-religionists, and by the menagerie keeper, who goes to the gladiators. The gladiators draw their swords nervously.

FERROVIUS. Lost! lost for ever! I have betrayed my Master. Cut off this right hand: it has offended. Ye have swords, my brethren: strike.

LAVINIA. No, no. What have you done, Ferrovius?

FERROVIUS. I know not; but there was blood behind my eyes; and theres blood on my sword. What does that mean?

THE EMPEROR [*enthusiastically, on the landing outside his box*] What does it mean? It means that you are the greatest man in Rome. It means that you shall have a laurel crown of gold. Superb fighter: I could almost yield you my throne. It is a record for my reign: I shall live in history. Once, in Domitian's time, a Gaul slew three men in the arena and gained his freedom. But when before has one naked man slain six armed men of the bravest and best? The persecution shall cease: if Christians can fight like this, I shall have none but Christians to fight for me. [*To the Gladiators*] You are ordered to become Christians, you there: do you hear?

RETIARIUS. It is all one to us, Caesar. Had I been there with my net, the story would have been different.

THE CAPTAIN [*suddenly seizing Lavinia by the wrist and dragging her up the steps to the Emperor*] Caesar: this woman is the sister of Ferrovius. If she is thrown to the lions he will fret. He will lose weight; get out of condition—

THE EMPEROR. The lions? Nonsense! [*To Lavinia*] Madam: I am proud to have the honor of making your acquaintance. Your brother is the glory of Rome.

LAVINIA. But my friends here. Must they die?

THE EMPEROR. Die! Certainly not. There has never been the slightest idea of harming them. Ladies and gentlemen: you are all free. Pray go into the front of the house and enjoy the spectacle to which your brother has so splendidly contributed. Captain: oblige me by conducting them to the seats reserved for my personal friends.

THE MENAGERIE KEEPER. Caesar: I must have one Christian for the lion. The people have been promised it; and they will tear the decorations to bits if they are disappointed.

THE EMPEROR. True, true: we must have somebody for the new lion.

FERROVIUS. Throw me to him. Let the apostate perish.

THE EMPEROR. No, no: you would tear him in pieces, my friend; and we cannot afford to throw away lions as if they were mere slaves. But we must have somebody. This is really extremely awkward.

THE MENAGERIE KEEPER. Why not that little Greek chap? He's not a Christian: he's a sorcerer.

THE EMPEROR. The very thing: he will do very well.

THE CALL BOY [*issuing from the passage*] Number twelve. The Christian for the new lion.

ANDROCLES [*rising, and pulling himself sadly together*] Well, it was to be, after all.

LAVINIA. I'll go in his place, Caesar. Ask the Captain whether they do not like best to see a woman torn to pieces. He told me so yesterday.

THE EMPEROR. There is something in that: there is certainly something in that—if only I could feel sure that your brother would not fret.

ANDROCLES. No: I should never have another happy hour.
No: on the faith of a Christian and the honor of a tailor, I accept
the lot that has fallen on me. If my wife turns up, give her my
love and say that my wish was that she should be happy with her
next, poor fellow! Caesar: go to your box and see how a tailor
can die. Make way for number twelve there. [*He marches out
along the passage*].

*The vast audience in the amphitheatre now sees the Emperor re-
enter his box and take his place as Androcles, desperately frightened,
but still marching with piteous devotion, emerges from the other end
of the passage, and finds himself at the focus of thousands of eager
eyes. The lion's cage, with a heavy portcullis grating, is on his left.
The Emperor gives a signal. A gong sounds. Androcles shivers at
the sound; then falls on his knees and prays. The grating rises with
a clash. The lion bounds into the arena. He rushes round frisking in
his freedom. He sees Androcles. He stops; rises stiffly by straighten-
ing his legs; stretches out his nose forward and his tail in a horizontal
line behind, like a pointer, and utters an appalling roar. Androcles
crouches and hides his face in his hands. The lion gathers himself for
a spring, swishing his tail to and fro through the dust in an ecstasy
of anticipation. Androcles throws up his hands in supplication to
heaven. The lion checks at the sight of Androcles's face. He then
steals towards him; smells him; arches his back; purrs like a motor
car; finally rubs himself against Androcles, knocking him over.
Androcles, supporting himself on his wrist, looks affrightedly at the
lion. The lion limps on three paws, holding up the other as if it was
wounded. A flash of recognition lights up the face of Androcles. He
flaps his hand as if it had a thorn in it, and pretends to pull the thorn
out and to hurt himself. The lion nods repeatedly. Androcles holds
out his hands to the lion, who gives him both paws, which he shakes
with enthusiasm. They embrace rapturously, finally waltz round the
arena amid a sudden burst of deafening applause, and out through
the passage, the Emperor watching them in breathless astonishment
until they disappear, when he rushes from his box and descends the
steps in frantic excitement.*

THE EMPEROR. My friends, an incredible! an amazing thing! has happened. I can no longer doubt the truth of Christianity. [*The Christians press to him joyfully*]. This Christian sorcerer— [*with a yell, he breaks off as he sees Androcles and the lion emerge from the passage, waltzing. He bolts wildly up the steps into his box, and slams the door. All, Christians and gladiators alike, fly for their lives, the gladiators bolting into the arena, the others in all directions. The place is emptied with magical suddenness*].

ANDROCLES [*naïvely*] Now I wonder why they all run away from us like that. [*The lion, combining a series of yawns, purrs, and roars, achieves something very like a laugh*].

THE EMPEROR [*standing on a chair inside his box and looking over the wall*] Sorcerer: I command you to put that lion to death instantly. It is guilty of high treason. Your conduct is most disgra—[*the lion charges at him up the stairs*] help! [*He disappears. The lion rears against the box; looks over the partition at him; and roars. The Emperor darts out through the door and down to Androcles, pursued by the lion*].

ANDROCLES. Dont run away, sir: he cant help springing if you run. [*He seizes the Emperor and gets between him and the lion, who stops at once*]. Dont be afraid of him.

THE EMPEROR. I am not afraid of him. [*The lion crouches, growling. The Emperor clutches Androcles*]. Keep between us.

ANDROCLES. Never be afraid of animals, your worship: thats the great secret. He'll be as gentle as a lamb when he knows that you are his friend. Stand quite still; and smile; and let him smell you all over just to reassure him; for, you see, he's afraid of you; and he must examine you thoroughly before he gives you his confidence. [*To the lion*] Come now, Tommy; and speak nicely to the Emperor, the great good Emperor who has power to have all our heads cut off if we dont behave very very respectfully to him.

The lion utters a fearful roar. The Emperor dashes madly up the steps, across the landing, and down again on the other side, with the lion in hot pursuit. Androcles rushes after the lion; overtakes him as he is descending; and throws himself on his back, trying to use his toes as a brake. Before he can stop him the lion gets hold of the trailing end of the Emperor's robe.

ANDROCLES. Oh bad wicked Tommy, to chase the Emperor like that! Let go the Emperor's robe at once, sir: wheres your manners? [*The lion growls and worries the robe*]. Dont pull it away from him, your worship. He's only playing. Now I shall be really angry with you, Tommy, if you dont let go. [*The lion growls again*]. I'll tell you what it is, sir: he thinks you and I are not friends.

THE EMPEROR [*trying to undo the clasp of his brooch*] Friends! You infernal scoundrel [*the lion growls*]—dont let him go. Curse this brooch! I cant get it loose.

ANDROCLES. We mustnt let him lash himself into a rage. You must shew him that you are my particular friend—if you will have the condescension. [*He seizes the Emperor's hands and shakes them cordially*]. Look, Tommy: the nice Emperor is the dearest friend Andy Wandy has in the whole world: he loves him like a brother.

THE EMPEROR. You little brute, you damned filthy little dog of a Greek tailor: I'll have you burnt alive for daring to touch the divine person of the Emperor. [*The lion growls*].

ANDROCLES. Oh dont talk like that, sir. He understands every word you say: all animals do: they take it from the tone of your voice. [*The lion growls and lashes his tail*]. I think he's going to spring at your worship. If you wouldnt mind saying something affectionate. [*The lion roars*].

THE EMPEROR [*shaking Androcles's hand frantically*] My dearest Mr Androcles, my sweetest friend, my long lost brother, come to my arms. [*He embraces Androcles*]. Oh, what an abominable smell of garlic!

The lion lets go the robe and rolls over on his back, clasping his forepaws over one another coquettishly above his nose.

ANDROCLES. There! You see, your worship, a child might play with him now. See! [*He tickles the lion's belly. The lion wriggles ecstatically*]. Come and pet him.

THE EMPEROR. I must conquer these unkingly terrors. Mind you dont go away from him, though. [*He pats the lion's chest*].

ANDROCLES. Oh, sir, how few men would have the courage to do that!

THE EMPEROR. Yes: it takes a bit of nerve. Let us have the Court in and frighten them. Is he safe, do you think?

ANDROCLES. Quite safe now, sir.

THE EMPEROR [*majestically*] What ho, there! All who are within hearing, return without fear. Caesar has tamed the lion. [*All the fugitives steal cautiously in. The menagerie keeper comes from the passage with other keepers armed with iron bars and tridents*]. Take those things away. I have subdued the beast. [*He places his foot on it*].

FERROVIUS [*timidly approaching the Emperor and looking down with awe on the lion*] It is strange that I, who fear no man, should fear a lion.

THE CAPTAIN. Every man fears something, Ferrovius.

THE EMPEROR. How about the Pretorian Guard now?

FERROVIUS. In my youth I worshipped Mars, the God of War. I turned from him to serve the Christian god; but today the Christian god forsook me; and Mars overcame me and took back his own. The Christian god is not yet. He will come when Mars and I are dust; but meanwhile I must serve the gods that are, not the God that will be. Until then I accept service in the Guard, Caesar.

THE EMPEROR. Very wisely said. All really sensible men agree that the prudent course is to be neither bigoted in our attachment to the old nor rash and unpractical in keeping an open mind for the new, but to make the best of both dispensations.

THE CAPTAIN. What do you say, Lavinia? Will you too be prudent?

LAVINIA [*on the stairs*] No: I'll strive for the coming of the God who is not yet.

THE CAPTAIN. May I come and argue with you occasionally?

LAVINIA. Yes, handsome Captain: you may. [*He kisses her hand*].

THE EMPEROR. And now, my friends, though I do not, as you see, fear this lion, yet the strain of his presence is considerable; for none of us can feel quite sure what he will do next.

THE MENAGERIE KEEPER. Caesar: give us this Greek sorcerer to be a slave in the menagerie. He has a way with the beasts.

ANDROCLES [*distressed*] Not if they are in cages. They should not be kept in cages. They must be all let out.

THE EMPEROR. I give this sorcerer to be a slave to the first man who lays hands on him. [*The menagerie keepers and the gladiators rush for Androcles. The lion starts up and faces them. They surge back*]. You see how magnanimous we Romans are, Androcles. We suffer you to go in peace.

ANDROCLES. I thank your worship. I thank you all, ladies and gentlemen. Come, Tommy. Whilst we stand together, no cage for you: no slavery for me. [*He goes out with the lion, everybody crowding away to give him as wide a berth as possible*].

* * * * *

In this play I have presented one of the Roman persecutions of the early Christians, not as the conflict of a false theology with a true, but as what all such persecutions essentially are: an attempt to suppress a propaganda that seemed to threaten the interests involved in the established law and order, organized and maintained in the name of religion and justice by politicians who are pure opportunist Have-and-Holders. People who are shewn by their inner light the possibility of a better world based on the demand of the spirit for a nobler and more abundant life, not for themselves at the expense of others, but for everybody, are naturally dreaded and therefore hated by the Have-and-Holders, who keep always in reserve two sure weapons against them. The first is a persecution effected by the provocation, organization, and arming of that herd instinct which makes men abhor all departures from custom, and, by the most cruel punishments and the wildest calumnies, force eccentric people to behave and profess exactly as other people do. The second is by leading the herd to war, which immediately and infallibly makes them forget everything, even their most cherished and hardwon public liberties and private interests, in the irresistible surge of their pugnacity and the tense preoccupation of their terror.

There is no reason to believe that there was anything more in the Roman persecutions than this. The attitude of the Roman Emperor and the officers of his staff towards the opinions at issue were much the same as those of a modern British Home Secretary towards members of the lower middle classes when some pious policeman charges them with Bad Taste, technically called blasphemy: Bad Taste being a violation of Good Taste, which in such matters practically means Hypocrisy. The Home Secretary and the judges who try the case are usually far more sceptical and blasphemous than the poor men whom they persecute; and their professions of horror at the blunt utterance of their own opinions are revolting to those behind the scenes who have any genuine religious sensibility; but the thing is done because the governing classes, provided only the law against blasphemy is not applied to themselves, strongly approve of such persecution because it enables them to represent their own privileges as part of the religion of the country.

Therefore my martyrs are the martyrs of all time, and my persecutors the persecutors of all time. My Emperor, who has no sense of the value of common people's lives, and amuses himself with killing as carelessly as with sparing, is the sort of monster you can make of any silly-clever-gentleman by idolizing him. We are still so easily imposed on by such idols that one of the leading pastors of the Free Churches in London denounced my play on the ground that my persecuting Emperor is a very fine fellow, and the persecuted Christians ridiculous. From which I conclude that a popular pulpit may be as perilous to a man's soul as an imperial throne.

All my articulate Christians, the reader will notice, have different enthusiasms, which they accept as the same religion only because it involves them in a common opposition to the official religion and consequently in a common doom. Androcles is a humanitarian naturalist, whose views surprise everybody. Lavinia, a clever and fearless freethinker, shocks the Pauline Ferrovius, who is comparatively stupid and conscience ridden. Spintho, the blackguardly debauchee, is presented as one of the typical Christians of that period on the authority of St Augustine, who seems to have come to the conclusion at one period of his development that most Christians were what we call wrong uns. No doubt he was to some extent right: I have had occasion often to point out that revolutionary movements attract those who are not good enough for established institutions as well as those who are too good for them.

But the most striking aspect of the play at this moment is the terrible topicality given it by the war. We were at peace when I pointed out, by the mouth of Ferrovius, the path of an honest man who finds out, when the trumpet sounds, that he cannot follow Jesus. Many years earlier, in The Devil's Disciple, I touched the same theme even more definitely, and shewed the minister throwing off his black coat for ever when he discovered, amid the thunder of the captains and the shouting, that he was a born fighter. Great numbers of our clergy have found themselves of late in the position of Ferrovius and Anthony Anderson. They have discovered that they hate not only their enemies but everyone who does not share their hatred, and that they want to fight and to force other people to fight. They have turned their churches into recruiting stations and their vestries into munition workshops. But it has never occurred to them to take off their black coats and say quite simply, "I find in the hour of trial that the Sermon on the Mount is tosh, and that I am not a Christian. I apologize for all the unpatriotic nonsense I have been preaching all these years. Have the goodness to give me a revolver and a commission in a regiment which has for its chaplain a priest of the god Mars: *my* God." Not a bit of it. They have stuck to their livings and served Mars in the name of Christ, to the scandal of all religious mankind. When the Archbishop of York behaved like a gentleman and the Head Master of Eton preached a Christian sermon, and were reviled by the rabble, the Martian parsons encouraged the rabble. For this they made no apologies or excuses, good or bad. They simply indulged their passions, just as they had always indulged their class prejudices and commercial interests, without troubling themselves for a moment as to whether they were Christians or not. They did not protest even when a body calling itself the Anti-German League (not having noticed, apparently, that it had been anticipated by the British Empire, the French Republic, and the Kingdoms of Italy, Japan, and Serbia) actually succeeded in closing a church at Forest Hill in which God was worshipped in the German language. One would have supposed that this grotesque outrage on the commonest decencies of religion would have provoked a remonstrance from even the worldliest bench of bishops. But no: apparently it seemed to the bishops as natural that the House of God should be looted when He allowed German to be spoken in it as that a baker's shop with a German name over the door should be pillaged. Their verdict was, in effect, "Serve God right, for creating the Germans!" The incident would have been impossible in a country where the Church was as powerful as the Church of England, had it had at the same time a spark of catholic as distinguished from tribal religion in it. As it is, the thing occurred; and as far as I have observed, the only people who gasped were the Freethinkers.

Thus we see that even among men who make a profession of religion the great majority are as Martian as the majority of their congregations. The average clergyman is an official who makes his living by christening babies, marrying adults, conducting a ritual, and making the best he can (when he has any conscience about it) of a certain routine of school superintendence, district visiting, and organization of almsgiving, which does not necessarily touch Christianity at any point except the point of the tongue. The exceptional or religious clergyman may be an ardent Pauline salvationist, in which case his more cultivated parishioners dislike him, and say that he ought to have joined the Methodists.

Or he may be an artist expressing religious emotion without intellectual definition by means of poetry, music, vestments, and architecture, also producing religious ecstasy by physical expedients, such as fasts and vigils, in which case he is denounced as a Ritualist. Or he may be either a Unitarian Deist like Voltaire or Tom Paine, or the more modern sort of Anglican Theosophist to whom the Holy Ghost is the Élan Vital of Bergson, and the Father and Son are an expression of the fact that our functions and aspects are manifold, and that we are all sons and all either potential or actual parents, in which case he is strongly suspected by the straiter Salvationists of being little better than an Atheist. All these varieties, you see, excite remark. They may be very popular with their congregations; but they are regarded by the average man as the freaks of the Church. The Church, like the society of which it is an organ, is balanced and steadied by the great central Philistine mass above whom theology looms as a highly spoken of and doubtless most important thing, like Greek Tragedy, or classical music, or the higher mathematics, but who are very glad when church is over and they can go home to lunch or dinner, having in fact, for all practical purposes, no reasoned convictions at all, and being equally ready to persecute a poor Freethinker for saying that St James was not infallible, and to send one of the Peculiar People to prison for being so very peculiar as to take St James seriously.

In short, a Christian martyr was thrown to the lions not because he was a Christian, but because he was a crank: that is, an unusual sort of person. And multitudes of people, quite as civilized and amiable as we, crowded to see the lions eat him just as they now crowd the lion-house in the Zoo at feeding-time, not because they really cared twopence about Diana or Christ, or could have given you any intelligent or correct account of the things Diana and Christ stood against one another for, but simply because they wanted to see a curious and exciting spectacle. You, dear reader, have probably run to see a fire; and if somebody came in now and told you that a lion was chasing a man down the street you would rush to the window. And if anyone were to say that you were as cruel as the people who let the lion loose on the man, you would be justly indignant. Now that we may no longer see a man hanged, we assemble outside the jail to see the black flag run up. That is our duller method of enjoying ourselves in the old Roman spirit. And if the Government decided to throw persons of unpopular or eccentric views to the lions in the Albert Hall or the Earl's Court stadium to-morrow, can you doubt that all the seats would be crammed, mostly by people who could not give you the most superficial account of the views in question. Much less unlikely things have happened. It is true that if such a revival does take place soon, the martyrs will not be members of heretical religious sects: they will be Peculiars, Anti-Vivisectionists, Flat-Earth men, scoffers at the laboratories, or infidels who refuse to kneel down when a procession of doctors goes by. But the lions will hurt them just as much, and the spectators will enjoy themselves just as much, as the Roman lions and spectators used to do.

It was currently reported in the Berlin newspapers that when Androcles was first performed in Berlin, the Crown Prince rose and left the house, unable to endure the (I hope) very clear and fair exposition of autocratic Imperialism given by the Roman captain to his Christian prisoners. No English Imperialist was intelligent and earnest enough to do the same in London. If the report is correct, I confirm the logic of the Crown Prince, and am glad to find myself so well understood. But I can assure him that the Empire which served for my model when I wrote Androcles was, as he is now finding to his cost, much nearer my home than the German one.

GENERAL INTRODUCTION TO THE WORKS OF BERNARD SHAW

By A. C. Ward

GEORGE BERNARD SHAW, the greatest of the many Irishmen who have written fine plays in the English language, was born in Dublin on 26 July 1856. His father, George Carr Shaw, the youngest son in a family of thirteen children, became a minor official in the Dublin law courts, but after a few years he retired on a small pension and went into business unsuccessfully as a corn merchant. He married the daughter of an Irish landowner, who soon found that her husband was a drunkard and incapable of earning enough money to provide for her and the three children who were born to them, George Bernard Shaw and his two sisters.

Mrs Shaw had a remarkably good singing voice, and from her and her friends young Bernard learned much good operatic music, and this was to be very useful to him afterwards. When he was sixteen his mother and sisters left Dublin and went to live permanently in London, where Mrs Shaw supported herself and her daughters by giving music lessons and singing at concerts.

In the meantime Bernard Shaw had been to school in Dublin until he was fifteen. He then became a clerk and cashier in a land agent's office there until April 1876, when he followed his mother to London. When he understood that his father was unqualified to be the controlling head of the family, and that his mother was more devoted to music than to her children, he developed that extraordinary independence of mind and spirit which was to enable him, later, to look upon mankind and its affairs without being swayed either by custom or by other people's conventional ideas of right and wrong.

Though he received little mother-love from Mrs Shaw, the love of music that he gained from her soon proved itself useful in London, where one of his first regular positions when he took up journalism was as music critic on the *Star*, a London evening newspaper. Both as a critic of music and, a few years later, as a critic of plays for the *Saturday Review*, a weekly periodical, he wrote essays of very high quality which are still read and praised, more than half a century after they were first printed.

When Shaw himself turned to the writing of plays, he heard with the inner ear of a musician the words that he set down to be spoken by the actors, and his sentences consequently run with a rhythmical ease that makes them easy and pleasant to speak and hear. It is for this reason that the many very long speeches in Shaw's plays are able to hold our attention, whereas speeches of a similar length by other modern playwrights are often tedious, even though the subjects they deal with may be as important as Shaw's. The finest example of the influence of opera on his dramatic work is Act III of *Man and Superman*, of which more will be said below.

After settling in London, Bernard Shaw found it very difficult to live by writing, and for the first ten years he had to rely mainly upon his mother for food and lodging. Yet during those years he was laying the foundations of his career, joining political societies and addressing public meetings, sometimes at street corners. One day in September 1884 he went to a hall in the City of London to hear a lecture by the American economist Henry George (author of a well-known book, *Progress and Poverty*) who advocated that national revenue should be raised by a single tax on land values, instead of by numerous taxes on a variety of things. Henry George's lecture converted Shaw to Socialism, and almost at once he joined the newly founded Fabian Society. The Fabians wanted to bring about a gradual evolutionary change, not a sudden and violent revolutionary one, from capitalism to socialism, and they had a powerful influence on British political life during the next forty or fifty years.

Round about the time Shaw joined the Fabian Society he also met Mrs Annie Besant, whose ardent support of independence for India did much to make the British public aware that the

Indian peoples' desire for political freedom could not be ignored. Mrs Besant was a great admirer of Shaw, and she soon joined him as a member of the Fabian Society, until her enthusiasm and energies were diverted to the support of Theosophy. She made herself the English leader of the theosophists and strengthened her ties with India through the theosophists there.

In his early years as a socialist Bernard Shaw believed that if the condition of civilized societies was to be improved, it must be done by legislation aiming at equality, reducing in various ways the fortunes of the rich in order to help and uplift the poor. Though he continued to preach equality for the remainder of his long life, as he grew older he trusted less in the power of Acts of Parliament to increase human welfare and happiness. He came round to the opinion that the first thing required in the making of a Good Society is not so much good laws as good men and women—men and women, that is, who are righteous in spirit and not merely well-intentioned and kind-hearted. Good people will make good laws, but good laws passed by a few do not necessarily make a good society.

While he was still a boy, Shaw had abandoned the Christian religion as it was practised by the churches, which he believed had strayed far from the teachings of Christ. But though he would not call himself a Christian, many of his strongest convictions and most of his personal conduct were those of a religious man. His sense of the sacredness of life, animal as well as human; his purity of living—he ate no flesh, drank no alcohol, smoked no tobacco; his kindness and generosity to his fellows (though he opposed charity on the ground that it was usually only a cheap substitute for social justice); his insistence that it is the duty of all men to strive to leave the world a better place than they found it, to hand on to future generations the torch of life burning more brightly—all these beliefs, though Shaw would have claimed that they were based on reason, not on faith, were so powerful in him as a guide to conduct that they had the force of a religion.

He became a vegetarian when he was twenty-five. His reading

L

of the works of the English poet Shelley had some influence in leading him to refrain from eating meat, but the stronger motive was his deep feeling that 'animals are our fellow creatures', not to be slain for human food.

Politics and journalism occupied Bernard Shaw until 1898, when he reached the age of forty-two. His first attempts at creative literary work produced five unsuccessful novels between 1879 and 1883, and in 1885 he made his first attempt to write a play, but left it unfinished. Seven years later he completed it and on 9 December 1892 it was performed in London. Called *Widowers' Houses*, this play dealt with the evils of London slums, in which at that time many filthy and decaying houses were owned by landlords who lived at ease elsewhere on the rents squeezed from poor and wretched tenants.

A play on such a subject—on, that is, a genuine social evil—was something entirely new in the English theatres. It had no success, and when in the following years Shaw went on to write other plays about real human problems, such as prostitution (*Mrs Warren's Profession*), war (*Arms and the Man*), religious intolerance (*The Devil's Disciple*), revenge (*Captain Brassbound's Conversion*), and so on, he was extremely unpopular with many people, and years were to pass before his plays brought him enough money to live on. For a gradually increasing number of people, however, he became a leader in new ways of thought and a champion of intellectual freedom.

Until Bernard Shaw began to write for the theatre, there had been no modern British dramatist who took current social, political, and religious problems as subjects for plays. He started out with the conviction that the emotional tangles of men and women had received far too much attention on the stage, and he made up his mind to do in English what Henrik Ibsen had been doing in Norwegian since about 1875; namely, to write plays discussing public affairs which touched the lives of very large numbers of people.

Not until a season of intellectual drama was started at the Court Theatre in London in 1904 were Bernard Shaw's plays brought to the notice of a large audience. The experiment was so successful that it continued until 1907, by which time there had been 711 performances of eleven of Shaw's plays there. *John Bull's Other Island* (a comedy about Irish politics) was the first play by Shaw that became popular.

It was at the same theatre that *Man and Superman* was produced on 23 May 1905. In the character of Henry Straker, the chauffeur, it introduced a new type of working man who understood and delighted in modern machinery and was destined to be more important in the technological age then approaching than the landed aristocracy who had for centuries been the ruling class. *Man and Superman*, called by Shaw 'A Comedy and a Philosophy', is full of ideas which were then new and startling, but we can only glance here at Act III, which is a kind of dream happening to some of the characters who appear in the first two acts. Act III introduces three persons from the old Spanish legend of Don Juan —Juan himself; Donna Anna, one of the many women he loved and betrayed; and the ghost of Anna's father, whom Don Juan had killed in a duel. They meet and converse with the Devil in Hell. Mozart, the great eighteenth-century Austrian composer, wrote an opera (*Don Giovanni*) based on the Don Juan legend, and the sounds of Mozart's music were in Bernard Shaw's ears while he was writing the many extremely long speeches for this scene in Hell, which begins where Mozart's opera ends. The opinions expressed by the four characters during their argument, which lasts for about ninety minutes in performance on the stage, were invented wholly by Shaw. It is often said that the characters in his plays are merely mouthpieces for Shaw's personal opinions, but this cannot be true, because in each of his plays the various characters put forward opinions which conflict with each other, and Shaw leaves the reader (or the spectator in the theatre) to decide which is right. In the 'Don Juan in Hell' scene the Devil tries to convince the others that human beings are so stupid and bad that nothing can save them from destruction. Don Juan claims that, on the contrary, there is in Man a spirit which inspires him to struggle upward towards the evolution of the Superman, who will be far wiser and better than Man is now. That spirit is named 'the Life Force' in Bernard Shaw's plays.

The discussion between the Devil and Don Juan and the others is a serious philosophical argument such as no other dramatist would have dared to write for the stage, since no one but Shaw would have thought it possible to make an audience listen to pure argument for so long. He succeeded, partly because he could be witty and amusing and make people laugh even while he was dealing with the most serious topics, and partly because he built up his great scenes just as a composer builds up the music in an opera or a symphony. Shaw introduces a subject for discussion, then another subject a little later on—as a composer brings in one musical theme or melody after another—and soon the various subjects are woven together into a discussion which interests us intellectually and pleases us artistically.

Shaw was always deeply interested in the *sound* of words as well as in their sense and meaning. As a young man he learned shorthand and always wrote his plays in it for his secretary to type out in longhand. This choice of shorthand as a working language was due both to its time-saving advantages and to its being based on phonetics, which always uses the same symbol for the same spoken sound. Ordinary written English is extremely illogical in spelling, a confusing variety of different sounds being represented by the same letters, *e.g.* cough = kof, but plough = plow, and dough = doh, etc. This makes English harder to learn and use than it might be if a separate letter or symbol were used for every sound. Shaw spent a good deal of time trying to persuade English people to adopt an enlarged alphabet. He also wrote one of his most popular plays, *Pygmalion*, on the subject of correct pronunciation, and he directed that after he died a considerable part of the large fortune he left should be used to finance any genuine scheme for bringing into common use his enlarged alphabet and reformed spelling. But the British have so far shown no inclination to adopt Bernard Shaw's system.

From 1905, when *Man and Superman*, his first great play, was performed, Shaw was the world's most famous living playwright, though he long remained unpopular with those who disliked his advanced views and his wish to reform society. Nevertheless it was at length widely recognized that he stood second only to Shakespeare among all the British playwrights, and his writings were known and valued in all countries long before he received the Nobel Prize for Literature in 1925.

Glimpses of the religious side of Shaw's nature appear in the majority of his plays, and very clearly in *Saint Joan*, where he took Joan of Arc both as a heroine of history and as a heroine of faith. She helped to free the land of France from the English armies in the fifteenth century, and she would obey only the voice of God which, she declared, spoke to her privately. She therefore refused to submit to the authority of priests and princes when they wanted her to behave contrary to what she believed God had told her, and she was burned as a heretic, as Shaw himself probably would have been if he had lived in Joan of Arc's century, for he had the same stubborn belief in the right of individual judgment based on the voice of conscience.

Though he did not enjoy foreign travel and went abroad very little—until his friends, especially his wife, persuaded him to visit Soviet Russia in 1931 and to go in 1932-3 on a voyage round the world, during which he visited Bombay—Shaw was in the widest sense an internationalist. In exile from his own land and living in England, for whose people he had curiously mixed feelings of affection, respect, and derision, he was without racial prejudices and looked on all nations with a cool and impartial eye. He did not care particularly for any one nation as a political unit, but he was benevolent to all humanity as a matter of principle. In his eyes most political leaders were blunderers, insufficiently educated in the art of ruling, which he regarded as the highest art of all.

In spite of his intense interest in political affairs, however, Shaw will almost certainly be remembered in the future much more by his plays than by his ideas on government and public affairs. He wrote fifty plays, long and short, but his other writings (which include *The Intelligent Woman's Guide to Socialism and Capitalism* and *Everybody's Political What's What*) are of much greater total length. The Prefaces which he added to most of the plays when they came to be printed are among the best prose essays that can be found anywhere in English literature, but their connection with the plays to which they are attached is often slight.

Shaw died in 1950, in his ninety-fifth year, having produced his last important play, *The Apple Cart*, some twenty years before, in 1929. The height of his fame was reached with *Saint Joan* in 1923, and it is most probable that this and several other of his plays will always be more highly thought of than *Back to Methuselah* (1922), which he himself regarded as his masterpiece.

Back to Methuselah, an enormously long work in five parts, fails as a play for more reasons than can be discussed within the limits of this Introduction. Its importance among Shaw's works comes from the clear statement of his 'gospel' in the Preface, and its working-out (much less clearly) in the dialogue of the five parts of the play. His gospel of Creative Evolution and his belief in the Life Force were opposed to Charles Darwin's theory of evolution by Natural Selection. In Darwin's theory the Survival of the Fittest comes about through the displacing of the weak by the strong, but the idea of Shaw's Creative Evolution is that the fittest are those who survive by superior intelligence and by the exercise of will power. Shaw held that if we desire with passionate strength of will to be better and finer people and to live longer, in fact to be changed into Supermen, and if that strength of will is passed on to our descendants, what we desire will ultimately be brought about. The nations would then be ruled in wisdom and virtue, and war and all other evils would vanish from the earth.

INTRODUCTION TO *ANDROCLES AND THE LION*

By A. C. Ward

THE FABLE of Androcles and the lion has been a favourite story since it was written down some eighteen hundred years ago by a Latin grammarian, Aulus Gellius, who was born—probably in Rome—about the year A.D. 123 and lived until about A.D. 165. He went to Greece and dwelt for a time near Athens, compiling while there a book in twenty sections called *Noctes Atticae* ('Attic Nights') from the fact that he wrote it on winter nights in Attica, the country in which Athens was the chief city.

In Bernard Shaw's play the old story is followed in outline so far as it concerns the encounter between the hurt lion and Androcles, but Shaw linked it on to an imaginary episode in the Roman persecution of the Christians, introduced argument and discussion bearing upon a few of the points dealt with in his Preface, and added knockabout fun to make it attractive to theatre audiences. This additional material turns the ancient fable into an original modern play which owes only a small debt to Gellius. It is a play, moreover, that only Shaw could have written, for no one but he would have ventured to combine comic nonsense with a serious study of religion.

While it would be easy to suggest that he was attracted to the legend of Androcles and the lion because he loved animals, such a suggestion would not be justified. Shaw was not an animal-lover of the kind that likes to keep animals in captivity as domestic pets, nor for exhibition in cages. He respected animals rather than loved them. To him they were as much God's creatures as human beings are: creatures to whom justice should be done by human beings, since animals are our fellow creatures.

Shaw was a lifelong vegetarian, partly because he felt a strong personal disgust towards the eating of dead flesh; but even if he could have enjoyed meat as a food he would still have refrained from it because of his conviction that it is altogether wrong to slaughter harmless and defenceless animals. Yet he would not for that reason have called himself an animal-lover. Indeed, it might be said that Shaw was not a lover either of animals or of human beings. He distrusted all emotional and sentimental relationships, regarding them as in most instances a form of enslavement which prevents full and independent development. A loved person or a loved animal often becomes a mere pet, and very few pets are allowed to live their own lives freely. To Shaw, justice and respect—which imply equality and freedom for all—were more desirable than the ill-defined range of feelings and sensations commonly called love.

He said in fun that his funeral would be attended not by coaches full of mourning men and women but 'by herds of oxen, sheep, swine, flocks of poultry, and a small travelling aquarium of live fish', in honour of the man who would rather have died than eat his fellow creatures.

Shaw was respectful and just to all living things. He did not eat animals, birds, or fish; neither did he consume human beings by subduing them to the pressure of his own emotions or his own convictions. He persuaded but never sought to compel others to accept his own views about the good life or the destiny of humanity. One of his most frequent quotations, and his own golden rule, was a saying attributed to Jesus in the New Testament (St. John's Gospel, ch. 10, v. 10): 'I am come that they might have life and have it more abundantly.' Shaw had no doubt that all men and women are bound in honour not only to live fully themselves but also to do their utmost to ensure that others have equal opportunity to live fully. He says in the Preface to this play that there are people 'who think a man is either alive or dead, and never consider the important question *how much alive* he is'. Poor people, or persecuted people, or those who are ruled by fear of any kind, were in his opinion only half alive.

Since religion is the main theme of this play and its Preface, it is necessary to understand that Shaw valued religion not according to the compulsive creed or theological doctrine of any particular religion, but according to whether or not it inspired people to strive for a better world, a world in which it will be possible for all to develop their individual powers unhampered by poverty, by class restrictions, or by mental and spiritual oppression.

The last words spoken by Androcles to the lion are significant: 'Whilst we stand together, no cage for you: no slavery for me.' Shaw was convinced that freedom—no cage, no slavery—is the absolute right of every creature. The Romans persecuted the Christians with varying degrees of severity for more than two hundred years, from the reign of Nero in the first century A.D. until Constantine became converted to Christianity early in the fourth century and made Christianity the State religion of the Empire. But almost as soon as they were relieved from persecution by the Romans, the Christians began to persecute one another as a consequence of differences of opinion about the nature and person of Jesus and about his teachings. The majority accepted doctrines and formulas of worship which became the fundamentals of belief and practice of the Christian Church centred in Rome with the Pope at its head. Any departure from official doctrine was treated as heresy, a word which means only 'contrary opinion' (originally it simply meant 'choice'); yet heresy was soon treated as sin and the worst of crimes, punishable by torture and death, as Shaw made plain in his *Saint Joan*.

The Christian Church (or Churches, for in the course of the centuries certain bodies of Christians have adopted beliefs opposed to those of the Church of Rome) has the proclaimed purpose of spreading throughout the world the teachings of Jesus, as these are interpreted by priests, or clergymen, or ministers. In the Preface to *Androcles and the Lion* Shaw suggests that the teachings of Jesus have for the most part been lost sight of, or even totally reversed, in western Christian civilization, and he examines the New Testament afresh in order to present his own conclusions about the personality of Jesus and the relevance to the modern world of Jesus's words and deeds as recorded by Matthew, Mark, Luke, and John. Shaw approached these writings in the same spirit of critical inquiry as he approached any other book. He read the New Testament 'without prejudice', neither as a worshipper of Christ nor as an antagonist. He did not accept the Christian belief that Jesus took upon himself the sins of all mankind, since Shaw was convinced that the consequences of human misdeeds are inescapable by mankind. He held that all the evidence of history goes to show that men suffer according to the ill-doing of themselves and others and that faith in a divine Redeemer cannot avert the penalties of ill-doing. He believed in the divinity of Jesus only in the degree that he believed in the divinity of all men, and in support of that belief Shaw cited Jesus's own words to those who questioned him: 'the kingdom of heaven is within you'.

It is impossible to reconcile Shaw's interpretation of the gospels with the interpretation of Christian believers, for he assumed that the worship of Jesus could be abandoned without loss and that attention should be concentrated upon Jesus as a real person who was chiefly concerned with the betterment of human behaviour, not with religious ceremonies or vows. But the Christian Church teaches that it is imperative to believe in Jesus as the Christ, the Son of God, the divine Saviour who, by allowing himself to be crucified, became a living sacrifice and thus saved from the consequences of sin all who accept him as Lord. The root principle of Christianity as Christians conceive of it is *faith* in the supernatural mission of Jesus. Shaw maintained, however, that *conduct* was the root principle of Jesus's teaching until he became obsessed by a delusion 'that he was himself a visible concrete God'. Although Shaw endeavoured to examine the New Testament gospels 'without prejudice' he was by nature incapable of doing so, for his rationalizing mind disabled him from accepting any supernatural element in a religion. What believers accept without question as supernatural and therefore beyond the scope of reason, he interpreted as myth, or the product of human imagination or credulity or self-deception.

For Shaw, therefore, the acceptable doctrines of Jesus could be summarized thus: (1) The kingdom of heaven is within you . . .

We are members one of another, and therefore unable to injure or help others without injuring or helping ourselves. . . . We are born and live to do God's work. (2) We must abolish private property and throw everything into the common stock, working for the work's sake, not for money. (3) We must get rid of punishment and revenge. (4) We must get rid of family ties which may hamper the doing of God's work.

Though he used the word God, Shaw rejected the idea of God as a person. He more frequently employed the term 'Life Force'— the vital spirit in mankind through which 'we evolve towards greater abundance of life'. At this point, Shaw's determination to arrive at a rational interpretation of the universe seems to break down, for reason cannot prove the existence of the Life Force. Acceptance of its reality as an operative power in human affairs is a matter of faith, even though it be of philosophical origin rather than a product of an established religious doctrine.

The numerous references in the *Androcles and the Lion* Preface to Jesus's teaching as a form of Communism require some clarification. At the time this Preface was written (1915) Communism was still an ideal political theory, not a system of government in practice as it has since become under the name of Marxism. It is no doubt necessary to describe the ideal commended by Shaw as 'pure Communism', for he was critical of Marx. Karl Marx, he writes in this Preface, was 'not content to take political economy as he found it', but 'insisted on rebuilding it from the bottom upwards in his own way, and thereby gave a new lease of life to the errors it was just outgrowing'. When, after 1918, Communism (or Marxism) attained power, it was before long, by a familiar irony of history, in the situation towards non-Communists that Shaw describes the Romans as being towards Christians. In the appendix to *Androcles and the Lion* he writes:

In this play I have presented one of the Roman persecutions of the early Christians, not as the conflict of a false theology with a true, but as all such persecutions essentially are: an attempt to suppress a propaganda that seemed to threaten the interests involved in the established law and order ... a persecution effected by the provocation, organization, and arming of that herd instinct which makes men abhor all departures from custom, and, by the most cruel punishments and the wildest calumnies, forces eccentric people to behave and profess exactly as other people do.

* * *

More than most of Shaw's plays *Androcles and the Lion* needs to be considered in close relation to its Preface if its serious purpose is not to be underestimated. When witnessed in performance on the stage it tends to appear slight and lacking in substance, whereas most of Shaw's other plays, both earlier and later than *Androcles*, are packed full with matter for thought and meditation, as well as with wit and humour: there is a balance between education and entertainment. In *Androcles and the Lion* that balance is upset, mainly because Shaw attempted the impossible by bringing on to the stage, in the figure of the lion, a mere make-believe character of the kind that audiences had become accustomed to in the farcical Christmas shows called pantomimes. Indeed, Shaw seems to have aimed to present *Androcles and the Lion* partly as though it were a pantomime, for in the Prologue Androcles himself and Megaera his wife closely resemble the comic characters of the meek husband and the scolding wife who commonly provided much of the rough fun in those Christmas shows, most of which were also based on old stories (*Cinderella, Beauty and the Beast, Ali Baba and the Forty Thieves*, etc.). But while the laughable parts of the Prologue are plain to all, the real point of the conversation between the husband and wife may be missed unless the uncomfortable relationship between them is understood as an illustration of what Shaw says in the Preface concerning the restrictive effects of marriage upon individual freedom: 'A married man ... will try to please his wife, and a married woman to please her husband, instead of doing the work of God.' On the other hand, a determination to do the work of God or to perform some imperative duty may prove to be inconsistent with pleasing the partner in marriage. Androcles, having become a Christian, and therefore finding himself bound to do God's work, finds the obligations of marriage to the unChristian Megaera impossible to reconcile with his Christian duty. This problem dissolves into uproarious farce, however, when the lion (*i.e.* an actor dressed up in an unrealistic stage costume) appears and brings the scene to a clowning end.

Even more is the balance upset by the lion's comic behaviour towards the end of the play, which obscures the serious theme of religious persecution and the necessity of obeying the voice of conscience.

But although in this play Shaw lapses from his usual high standard of skill as a playwright, the incongruous element of farce is not unintentional. From the beginning of his career in the theatre, more than twenty years earlier, Shaw had deliberately set himself to avoid solemnity in his treatment of important subjects. He held, rightly, that a theatre audience will not listen attentively to serious argument unless this is offered in an entertaining form lightened with wit and humour. Solemnity may quickly degenerate into dull heaviness, and then the audience's attention wanders and boredom creeps in. Shaw's triumph as a dramatist, and his superiority over his imitators, lay in his ability to communicate serious ideas so entertainingly that even unwilling audiences found themselves silently entranced. Yet this method of communication brought its own risks, and Shaw's dramatic tact was not always proof against an inclination to offset seriousness by triviality, as happens in parts of *Androcles and the Lion*.

Another cause of the relative failure of this play is that the characters do not 'come to life' as individual men and women. They are little more than *types*, set to express attitudes and points of view. Shaw acknowledges this in the appendix, where he describes Lavinia as 'a clever and fearless freethinker', Ferrovius as 'comparatively stupid and conscience ridden', and Spintho as a 'blackguardly debauchee'. They are just that and nothing but that, whereas in Shaw's other plays on religious themes—*e.g. Fanny's*

First Play and *Saint Joan*—the characters have independent life. We feel that they might do or say something unexpected and surprising; that they might at any moment cease to obey the author's orders and go beyond his original intentions and speak and behave according to some inner law of their own nature. Unless some such possibility is always latent in a play it has little of the dramatic tension which is necessary to keep the audience alert. It is a baffling but fascinating paradox of all imaginative literature that although an author needs to be in full control of his material, he must nevertheless create the illusion that his characters have a measure of the individual freedom of thought and action which Shaw insisted was the birthright of all created things.

GENERAL NOTE

Shaw introduced certain peculiarities in the printing of the dialogue of his plays. He omitted the apostrophe in such spoken contractions as itll (see page 109), usually printed it'll (= it will); and instead of *italic type* for emphasized words he used s p a c e d l e t t e r s (see, *e.g.*, page 123: Does that comfort you?).

For the assistance of students in other countries who have not constant access to dictionaries and other necessary reference books, the Notes in the following pages include definitions and explanations of various words and phrases which will be already familiar to English-born readers.

NOTES ON THE PREFACE TO
ANDROCLES AND THE LION

1. *Barabbas:* the thief who was released instead of Jesus: see St
John's Gospel (ch. 18, v. 40) in the New Testament. In St
Mark's Gospel (ch. 15, v. 7) and St Luke's (ch. 23, v. 18)
Barabbas is described as a rebel and murderer: compare with
St Matthew's Gospel (ch. 27, vv. 16–26). Shaw uses the name
here to signify all those in nations and churches whom he re-
garded as having ignored or misinterpreted the teachings of
Jesus.

'This man': Jesus.

taken his cross as a standard: Since Jesus was crucified, the cross on
which he died has become the Christian symbol of his sacrifice.
Shaw believed that this symbol had often been adopted hypo-
critically by those who professed to be followers of Jesus
although their principles and conduct were contrary to his.

the right end of it: To 'get hold of the right end of the stick' is an
idiomatic phrase meaning that a certain thing has been rightly
done or properly understood.

the Kingdom of God in Munster: In 1533. John of Leyden (see
note to p. 2 below) went as a missionary to Münster, in Prussia,
and became the leader of a large body of religious enthusiasts
who were called 'the saints'. John became King of Münster for a
year, but was then overthrown by the bishop, tortured, and
executed.

2. *Pilate:* the Roman procurator (magistrate, or governor) of Judaea
(A.D. 26–36); he was the judge before whom Jesus was tried.

Annas and Caiaphas: the Jewish high priests who sent Jesus for
trial.

Savonarola: Fra Girolamo Savonarola (1452–98), Italian monk of
the Order of St Dominic; he was a fanatical preacher and democratic leader in the city of Florence, and these activities led to his
being condemned and executed for heresy.

John of Leyden: Johann Beuckels (1509–36), originally a tailor and
later an innkeeper in the Dutch town of Leyden, before he made
himself the leader of 'the saints' in Münster (see note to p. 1
above).

2. *scuttling the ship:* sinking a ship by making holes in its sides or bottom, usually to prevent its falling into enemy hands. Shaw uses the phrase here to suggest that Savonarola and John of Leyden attempted to destroy existing political systems without offering adequate alternatives.

wearing a beard, working in a carpenter's shop: most artists' (imaginary) portraits of Jesus show him with a beard; his mother's husband is said to have been a carpenter.

believing that the earth is flat: in ancient times and by many in the Middle Ages this was believed; the discovery that it is a globe revolving round the sun was for long regarded as a heresy by the Christian Church.

3. *Tolstoy:* Count Leo Tolstoy (1828–1910), Russian novelist, essayist, and playwright. After a sinful early life he became deeply religious, advocated non-resistance to evil, and renounced his wealth and estates. His ideas and principles had considerable influence in Russia and elsewhere, and his *War and Peace* is regarded by many as the greatest novel ever written.

the Greek Church: otherwise known as the Orthodox Church or the Eastern Church; it separated from the Roman Church in A.D. 1054 owing to certain differences in doctrine and its refusal to accept the supremacy of the Pope. Its head is the Patriarch and its followers are mainly in Greece, Russia, and neighbouring countries.

Confucius: Chinese philosopher (*c.* 550–478 B.C.), whose wise 'sayings' were the basis of Confucianism, an ethical system with a deep and widespread influence in China until the fall of the empire there. His chief principle was expressed as 'Do not unto others what you would not wish done unto yourself.'

Alexander: Alexander the Great (356–323 B.C.), Greek military leader and conqueror of the Persians. His expeditions took him to Egypt (where he founded Alexandria) and to India.

Augustus: the title given to Caius Julius Caesar Octavianus (63 B.C.–A.D. 14), nephew of the great Julius Caesar. He became the first Roman emperor in 27 B.C. and later emperors also assumed the title of Augustus.

recalcitrance: unwillingness to conform to authority or custom.

4. *inculcated:* imposed by frequent and long-continued teaching.

Mahomet: Muhammad, or Mohammed (*c.* A.D. 570–632), the

Prophet and founder of the Moslem religion (Islam), whose revelations are set down in the Koran (Quran).

4. *John the Baptist:* the desert prophet who preached in Judaea and baptized Jesus (see St Matthew's Gospel, ch. 3).

British bulldog contempt: The bulldog is traditionally regarded as symbolizing the immovable determination of the British character.

Secularist: a person who rejects supernatural religion and accepts no faith that cannot be approved by reason.

Colonel Roosevelt: Theodore Roosevelt (1858–1919), President of the United States of America from 1901 to 1908. He was a distant relative of the later President, Franklin Delano Roosevelt.

Admiral von Tirpitz Alfred Peter Friedrich von Tirpitz (1849–1930), an eminent German naval commander and a principal founder of the modern German navy from 1897 to 1914, during which period he was Secretary of State for the Navy.

Simon Peter: one of the twelve disciples chosen by Jesus, after whose death he became a chief apostle. He is believed to have ended his missionary journeys in Rome and to have been executed there in the reign of the emperor Nero. As St Peter he is regarded as the founder of the Christian (Roman Catholic) Church.

5. *'Gentle Jesus, meek and mild':* an English hymn written in 1742 by Charles Wesley (1707–88), brother of John Wesley the founder of the Methodists, a Nonconformist offshoot of the Church of England, who have become one of the largest Christian bodies.

snivelling: feeble and tearful; whining.

Judas Maccabeus: a leader of the Jews in their revolt against oppression by the Syrians. He died in 160 B.C.

everybody's butt: a person of weak or extremely sensitive character who is tormented and ridiculed.

nincompoop: a feeble person of no importance.

Galileo: Galileo Galilei (1564–1642), Italian astronomer and physicist who made important discoveries. For agreeing with the view of Copernicus (1473–1543) that the earth moves round the sun he was imprisoned and compelled by the Church to retract, but in his famous saying *eppur si muove* ('nevertheless it moves') he refuted the orthodox dogma that the earth was stationary.

M

NOTES ON THE PREFACE

6. *a Primate:* an archbishop; *e.g.* the Archbishop of Canterbury has the rank of Primate of All England.

Eton: the leading public school in England.

Victoria Cross: a military decoration introduced (1856) by Queen Victoria and awarded to any officer or man serving in the British armed services for deeds of exceptional valour.

7. *Authorized Version:* an English translation of the Bible which has been used more than any other since it was first published in 1611.

Ulster: one of the four provinces of Ireland; the main part is now called Northern Ireland, which has its own government but remains in close association with Britain and continues to send members to the Parliament at Westminster.

Goethe: Johann Wolfgang von Goethe (1749–1832), Germany's greatest poet. His dramatic poem *Faust* (Part I, 1808; II, 1832), started about 1770, is the most famous treatment of the medieval legend.

could not stick it: English colloquial phrase meaning 'could not endure it' or 'could not get to the end of it'.

8. *Wesley:* John Wesley (1703–91), Christian preacher and founder of the Methodists (see note to p. 5 above, under 'Gentle Jesus . . .'). He is regarded as one of the originators of the Evangelical Revival which stirred England in the later part of the eighteenth century and was largely responsible for the social reforms which followed by slow degrees in later generations.

Tom Paine: Thomas Paine (1737–1809), English writer on politics and religion. In *The Rights of Man* (1791–2) he replied to Burke's *Reflections on the French Revolution* (1790), putting forward views then alarmingly revolutionary but since adopted for the most part in British legislation. In *The Age of Reason* (1793) Paine attacked Christianity, and many orthodox people still regard him as a dangerous influence.

Mr Worldly Wiseman: a character in *The Pilgrim's Progress* (1678), a religious allegory by John Bunyan (1628–88).

St Paul: originally named Saul, when he was one of the persecutors of the Christians. After becoming converted to their faith he became the chief apostle and in the view of some critics fostered a form of Christianity different from that taught by Jesus.

8. *Plymouth Brother:* a member of the religious body of strict
   Christians started in England at Plymouth about 1830. They
   believe wholly in the Bible as a guide to faith and conduct, hold
   aloof from worldly amusements and indulgences, and have no
   priests or ordained ministers.

   Philistines: originally a people who lived in a part of Palestine and
   were at enmity with the Israelites. Now applied to any body of
   persons antagonistic to the beliefs or culture of others.

9. *Knipperdolling:* Bernhard Knipperdolling (died 1536), a supporter
   of John Leyden in Münster (see notes to pp. 1 and 2 above).
   He was executed when the town was recaptured.

   Saracen: those peoples of the eastern lands who fought against the
   Christian Crusaders were called Saracens, a word of obscure
   origin.

   Crusader: the Crusades (Wars of the Cross), a series of expeditions
   in the eleventh-thirteenth centuries which began with the
   ostensible purpose of recovering by the Christians the Holy
   Land, which was then under the control of Islam.

   Kant: Immanuel Kant (1724–1804), German philosopher.

11. *The Baronet's cousin:* Volumnia Dedlock, cousin of Sir Leicester
    Dedlock, in *Bleak House* (1853), a novel by Charles Dickens
    (1812–70). In ch. 53 she makes the remark quoted by Shaw.

    Cain: one of the two sons of Adam and Eve (Book of Genesis,
    ch. 4) and the murderer of his younger brother Abel.

12. *shekels:* A shekel was a Jewish silver coin; the plural of the word is
    now applied, as slang or in contempt, to any sum of money.

13. *Baldur the Beautiful:* the son of Odin the sun god in Scandinavian
    mythology.

    Luther and Calvin: Martin Luther (1483–1546), German theo-
    logian and leader of the Protestant Reformation; Johannes
    Calvin (1509–64), French theologian and reformer, whose
    strict discipline and harsh doctrine have caused 'Calvinism' to
    become a word suggesting a joyless faith. Calvin's *Institutes of
    the Christian Religion* (1535) is a theological masterpiece.

    casuistry: subtle intellectual argument, usually connected with
    religious dogma, and directed to the purpose of proving the
    truth of statements which others consider contrary to reason.

14. *Frazer's Golden Bough:* a work in eleven volumes (1890–1915),
    surveying by the comparative method the beliefs of mankind at

various times and in various parts of the world, by Sir James
Frazer (1854–1941), Scottish anthropologist.

14. *John Barleycorn:* the grain of barley is personified in folklore
under this name, with the significance indicated by Shaw in the
passage which follows in his Preface.

Cecil Sharp: (1859–1924) English composer and collector of folk
songs, which he published in several volumes.

magnum opus: an author's (or composer's) greatest work (Latin).

eating a beefsteak: Shaw was a vegetarian and prejudiced against
all eating of meat.

16. *Apollo:* in Greek mythology, the sun god.

the Tichborne claimant: in 1872 an impostor named Arthur Orton
claimed to be the true heir to the valuable estates of the Tichborne family. He brought an action in the English law courts,
pretending that he was really Roger Charles Tichborne, who
had in fact been drowned at sea in 1854, aged twenty-five. The
case excited great public interest and controversy between those
who believed the claimant's story and those who were not
deceived by it. After Orton had lost the suit, he was charged
with perjury and sent to prison.

17. *the evangelists:* Matthew, Mark, Luke, and John.

18. *Holinshed:* Ralph (or Raphael) Holinshed (died about 1580). The
Chronicles (more or less legendary histories of England, Scotland, and Ireland) known by his name were partly the work of
others. Issued in 1577 and 1586, they were used by Shakespeare
as source material for certain of his plays, including *Macbeth*.

Froissart: Jean Froissart (c. 1337–1410), French historian, whose
Chronicles deal (with limited accuracy) with events in several
countries during three-quarters of a century (1325–1400). Lord
Berners translated them into English (1523–5).

Benvenuto Cellini: (1500–1571), Italian goldsmith and sculptor
who produced magnificent works in those arts, but is now more
widely remembered for his lively *Autobiography*, published
in Italy in 1730 and in several English translations at later
dates.

19. *transubstantiation:* the Roman Catholic doctrine that the bread
and wine administered by the priest to believers in the rite of
the Mass are converted absolutely into the body and blood of
Christ. This doctrine was discarded by the leaders of the Pro-

testant Reformation in the sixteenth century, and the bread and wine are still regarded only symbolically by the Protestant Churches.

20. *chaffing:* teasing or making fun of.

teetotaller: a person who abstains entirely from intoxicating drink.

wine-bibber: a person who drinks wine too frequently.

straitlaced: narrow-minded; rigidly moral; prudish.

21. *jocular:* light-hearted; merry; disposed to make jokes.

poohpoohs: has a low opinion of.

Samuel Butler: 1835–1902, English satirist, essayist, and writer on Evolution; the book Shaw alludes to here is *Erewhon* (1872).

Bunyan: John Bunyan (1622–88), author of *The Pilgrim's Progress* (1678) and other religious allegories.

a Bohemian: a person who pays no regard to conventional standards of conduct.

22. *Punch:* the chief character in the traditional Punch and Judy puppet play.

Til Eulenspiegel: a comic character in a series of German traditional tales published in 1519 and possibly based on the sly exploits of an actual person, of peasant origin, born about 1300.

23. *charlatan:* a cheat; one who pretends to have powers or abilities which he does not possess.

Rousseau: Jean-Jacques Rousseau (1712–78), French political philosopher whose views expressed in *The Social Contract* (1762) helped to prepare the way for the French Revolution. He also wrote on the principles of education in *Émile* (1762) and, as Shaw's reference shows, on religious topics.

24. *cataract:* a serious disease affecting the eyes and curable only by a delicate surgical operation.

30. *Keir Hardie:* James Keir Hardie (1856–1915), Scottish miner who became a Socialist politician and Member of Parliament.

of the Ruskin-Morris class: John Ruskin (1819–1900), writer on art and political economy; William Morris (1834–96), poet, artist, craftsman, and Socialist; both belonged to the well-to-do classes.

monomaniac: a person obsessed by a single idea.

Plato: one of the two greatest ancient Greek philosophers, the other being Aristotle. He lived from 428 to 347 B.C. and was a pupil of Socrates (469–399 B.C.) the substance of whose teaching is known through Plato's *Dialogues* and Xenophon's *Memorabilia*.

32. *paleographers:* experts on ancient manuscripts and inscriptions.

33. *Chauvinist:* excessively patriotic. The word comes from the name of Nicholas Chauvin, a French soldier of the Napoleonic period who made himself ridiculous by his bombastic patriotism.

Tarpeian rock: Tarpeia, the daughter of a Roman governor, treacherously admitted the enemies to the city, whereupon the invaders slew her. The place of her death became known as 'the Tarpeian rock' and criminals were executed by being thrown from it. The phrase is applied to any similar place of execution.

34. *Dame aux Camellias:* the repentant prostitute in a play with that title by the French dramatist Alexandre Dumas the younger (1824–95).

Charles Surface: the carefree young hero in *The School for Scandal* (1777), a famous comedy by Richard Brinsley Sheridan (1751–1816).

Des Grieux: the hero of *Manon Lescaut* (1731), a French novel by the Abbé Prévost (1697–1763).

Lourdes: a town in southern France with a sacred grotto which is a place of pilgrimage for Roman Catholics, who believe that miraculous cures are effected in a spring of water there.

35. *thaumaturgic:* miraculous; magical.

37. *Madagascar:* a large island off the east coast of Africa.

synoptic: providing a general survey or summary.

sophisticated: subtle-minded; lacking simplicity.

urbane: having polished manners; elegantly polite.

38. *a sop:* a piece of bread dipped in wine (or, ordinarily, in water or broth).

publican: as used in the New Testament, a tax-collector.

39. *codices:* (plural of *codex*), ancient manuscripts.

hedged: avoided a straightforward statement of.

40. *verisimilitude:* appearance of truth.

divinatory: inspired.

idiosyncrasies: a person's special and peculiar characteristics.

the 82nd Psalm: in the Old Testament; Shaw refers to verses 3, 4, and 6—'Defend the poor and fatherless: do justice to the afflicted and needy. Deliver the poor and needy: rid them out of the hand of the wicked. . . . I have said, Ye are gods; and all of you are children of the most High.'

41. *a fortiori:* more certainly (Latin).

42. *consensus:* general agreement of opinion.

43. *elderly wrangles:* long-continued and bad-tempered argument.

subjective: governed by personal feelings or prejudices.

battle of Waterloo: fought at the place of that name in Belgium in 1815; it brought the Napoleonic wars to an end, the French under Napoleon Bonaparte being defeated by the British and allied armies under the Duke of Wellington.

a large body of Russian troops: a false report was spread and widely believed that Russian soldiers had been seen travelling by train through England on their way to fight against the Germans in France.

Pompey: Gnaeus Pompeius (106–48 B.C.), Roman general who fought against Julius Caesar in the civil war (49–48 B.C.); when defeated he fled to Egypt and was stabbed to death by one of his former officers.

Church of Christ Scientist: the official name of the Christian Science churches founded in America by Mrs Mary Baker Eddy (1821–1910); it teaches through her book *Science and Health* (1875 and later editions) that man is a spiritual creature and that disease has no real existence but is a form of error to be overcome by mental power.

44. *that Shakespear was Bacon:* The universal genius of Shakespear's plays has persuaded certain people that they could not have been written by anyone but a university-educated man. Several names have been put forward as that of the 'true' author, that of Francis (Lord) Bacon being the favourite. Those who believe in this theory suggest that because playwriting was not then a gentlemanly occupation, Bacon used Shakespear's name instead of his own. Comparison of the plays with Bacon's acknowledged philosophical writings and essays gives no support to the theory, which was started in the eighteenth century, more than two hundred years after Shakespear's death.

angels . . . at the battle of Mons: a legend of the first World War. When the British forces were driven back by the Germans at Mons in Belgium in 1914, a story was circulated that angels were seen leading and protecting them during the retreat. Superstitious people believed it as a fact, but the story was originated by an imaginative writer.

44. *boggle at:* find it impossible to believe in.

St Januarius: a bishop killed during the persecution of Christians in the reign of the Roman emperor Diocletian (A.D. 245–313). His head and dried blood are preserved as religious relics in the Italian city of Naples, and the blood is believed by Roman Catholics to become liquid again at particular times each year.

elixir of life, transmuters of metals: It was believed in the Middle Ages that a potion could be discovered possessing the power of giving immortal life, and that base metals could be turned into gold if the right transmuting substance (called 'the philosopher's stone') were found.

the Newtons and Leibnitzes: Sir Isaac Newton (1642–1727), English mathematical philosopher and discoverer of the law of gravitation. 'Newtonian physics' remained unquestioned until Einstein announced the theory of Relativity in 1916. Gottfried Wilhelm Leibnitz (1646–1716), German mathematical philosopher who discovered simultaneously but independently certain mathematical principles published in Newton's Method of Fluxions (1704).

45. *Charles's Wain:* the popular name for the group of stars forming the constellation of Ursa Major or the Great Bear. 'Charles' in this connection may be derived from Charles the Great (Charlemagne) (A.D. 742–814), Emperor of the West, through some legendary association. Wain = farm wagon, the stars referred to being in a pattern resembling the outline of a cart. This group of stars is also called by some 'the Plough'.

Seven deadly sins: in medieval belief these were Pride, Lechery, Envy, Anger, Covetousness, Gluttony, and Sloth.

seven swords of sorrow in the heart of the Virgin: the pangs of sorrow supposed to have been felt at various times by the mother of Jesus, who is called the Virgin Mary. According to Roman Catholic belief the seven sorrows she experienced were: at the prophecy of Simeon (see St Luke's Gospel, ch. 2, vv. 25–35); at the flight of the holy family into Egypt; at the loss of the child Jesus; on meeting Jesus on the road to Calvary; on standing at the foot of the cross on which he died; on the taking down of his body from the cross; at his burial.

45. *seven champions of Christendom:* in a sixteenth-century romance by Richard Johnson (1573–?1659), *The Famous Historie of the Seven Champions of Christendom (c.* 1597), these are St George (England), St Denis (France), St James (Spain), St Anthony (Italy), St Andrew (Scotland), St Patrick (Ireland), and St David (Wales).

William the Conqueror: William, Duke of Normandy, became King William I of England in 1066 after defeating King Harold at the battle of Hastings. He lived from 1027 to 1087.

The Kaiser: Wilhelm II, Emperor of Germany from 1888 until he abdicated in 1918 when Germany was defeated in the first World War.

46. *annular:* shaped like a ring.

an Ulster Protestant: A large majority of the people of Northern Ireland, which forms part of the province of Ulster, are Protestant Christians, whereas in the remainder of Ireland Roman Catholics predominate. The Ulster Protestants are, in general, passionately anti-Catholic.

St Thomas Aquinas: (1227–74), the greatest of Catholic theologians; the son of an Italian nobleman, he became, and chose to remain all his life, a poor Dominican monk and religious teacher and writer. His *Summa Theologica* is a famous work on all human knowledge in relation to the Christian religion.

Sir Almroth Wright: (1861–1947), English physician and pathologist (*i.e.* a specialist in the scientific study of disease and its causes); he originated systems of inoculation against disease and methods for measuring disease-resisting substances present as a natural protective in human blood. These theories and practices are discussed by the characters in Bernard Shaw's *The Doctor's Dilemma* (1906), Sir Colenso Ridgeon in that play being an imaginative portrait of Sir Almroth Wright, who was one of Shaw's friends.

streptococci: a kind of disease germs or bacteria which are chain-like in shape when seen magnified under a microscope.

serum: a thin transparent fluid which forms part of the blood; but the word is now more commonly used in reference to the fluid injected into patients, and containing a substance which fights against or prevents disease.

the number of angels ... on the point of a needle: in medieval scholastic disputations (a formal type of debate conducted according to strict principles of logic) such a subject as this might be chosen for discussion as a religious and intellectual exercise.

46. *Bacon:* Francis, Lord Bacon (1561–1626), English philosopher and statesman. See also note to p. 44 above, on Shakespear and Bacon.

Montaigne: Michel D'Eyquem, Sieur de Montaigne (1533–92), French essayist and magistrate. His essays (1580 and later editions) are among the world's greatest books, full of wisdom and wit, friendly and often humorous in tone, but also often concerned with problems of life and death.

Cervantes: Miguel de Cervantes Saavedra (1547–1616), Spanish novelist and playwright; most famous as the author of the comic and satirical romance, *Don Quixote de la Mancha* (1605, 1615).

the Venerable Bede: (673–735), English religious scholar and historian; his *Ecclesiastical History of the English People* (written in Latin) is a valuable account of the period from 55 B.C. to A.D. 731.

Piers Plowman: a long poem, *The Vision concerning Piers Plowman,* by William Langland (?1330–?1400); written between, probably, 1360 and 1390. Next to *The Canterbury Tales* by Geoffrey Chaucer it is the most important English poem of that period, and much more serious in tone than Chaucer's.

Aristotle: one of the two greatest ancient Greek philosophers, the other being Plato; he lived from 384 to 322 B.C.

47. *artificial respiration:* a method for restoring the breathing of an apparently dead person by movements which alternately expand and contract the lungs; mostly used in cases of apparent drowning.

Theosophists: believers in Theosophy, a philosophical-religious system which assumes the existence of God as a spiritual essence penetrating the entire universe and the source of all life and all good, evil being assumed as of men's creation through their passion for material things.

iconolatry: worship of images (statues and pictures) of Jesus or other holy personages.

iconoclast: a person who destroys such images or actively opposes the worship of them; also applied now to anyone who attacks any commonly held belief.

47. *Methodist:* The Methodists are a religious body founded mainly by John Wesley (see note to p. 3 above).

48. *Bunyan's riddle:* lines in *The Pilgrim's Progress*:

> A man there was, tho' some did count him mad,
> The more he cast away, the more he had.

Don Juan: a Spanish legendary character who first appeared in literature in *El Burlador de Sevilla y convidado* (The Trickster of Seville and the Guest of Stone) written in 1630 by Tirso de Molina, a monk whose real name was Gabriel Tellez. Since then the Don Juan story has been used by many other writers in differing versions, the most popular being those which present Juan as a great lover and deceiver of women, including Donna Anna whose father he killed in a duel. In mockery Juan invites the statue of the dead man to supper and, the invitation having been accepted, Juan is afterwards dragged down to hell. In Shaw's play *Man and Superman* (published 1903) the legend is very differently treated.

Judaism, Mahometanism, Shintoism: the religions of Israel, Islam, and Japan (where Buddhism has weakened the hold of Shintoism).

Fire Worship: it is popularly though inaccurately supposed that in India the Parsees are fire-worshippers; their reverence for fire is only one aspect of their general reverence for the other primary forces in Nature.

49. *the present war:* the first World War of 1914–18.

the Life Force: Shaw's name for the driving power or animating spirit in men and women which he believed compelled the best among them to strive continuously for human betterment which would lead finally to the achievement of a nobler creature, the Superman. He developed this idea mainly in *Man and Superman* (1903) and *Back to Methuselah* (1920).

nimbus: the disc or ring which encircles the head of a divine or saintly personage in Christian pictures and statues.

50. *Mammon:* originally the Aramaic word for riches, but now used as a proper name for an imaginary god of money.

51. *stockbroker:* a dealer in the stocks and shares of commercial and industrial companies, and in government bonds and securities.

prima facie: a Latin term used here in the sense of 'immediate'.

spree: a noisy party.

51. *Reformation:* the religious movement begun by Martin Luther (1483–1546), the German theologian, for the reform of the Christian Church as it then existed under the Pope's control. It developed throughout Western Europe in a way which led to to the formation of national Protestant Churches (such as the Church of England) which declared themselves independent of the hitherto universal Church of Rome.

Renascence: (more usually spent *Renaissance*): the revival or re-birth of Learning which began in Italy in the fourteenth century with Dante and others and had spread throughout Western Europe by the sixteenth century.

the commercial night of the nineteenth century: in Shaw's opinion the general commercial prosperity in the nineteenth century was accompanied by a serious decline in spiritual and ethical values.

make men good by Act of Parliament: in his later life Shaw would in all probability have modified his statement here that men could be made good only by Act of Parliament. Though he continued to believe that social justice must be established in that way, he came to recognize that real goodness—of heart, mind, and spirit—depended upon other factors: see, *e.g.*, 'What is My Religious Faith?' in Shaw's autobiographical volume *Sixteen Self Sketches* (1949).

Chancellor of the Exchequer: the official title of the British minister of finance.

52. *Robinson Crusoe:* the hero of the novel *The Life and Strange Surprising Adventures of Robinson Crusoe* (1719), by Daniel Defoe (?1660–1731).

Juan Fernandez: an island in the Pacific Ocean on which a Scottish sailor, Alexander Selkirk, lived alone from 1704 to 1709. The accounts of Selkirk's experiences on the uninhabited island led Defoe to write *Robinson Crusoe*.

Nero: (A.D. 37–68); Roman emperor from A.D. 54 until his death. He was of evil reputation and accused of many crimes, including murder and the destruction of Rome by fire (A.D. 64), but it is difficult to separate fact from falsehood in connection with his reign. The story that 'he fiddled while Rome was burning' (*i.e.* played a musical instrument while watching with cruel satisfaction the doomed city) may be only a slander started by his enemies. He nevertheless created much hatred and fear, and when he was at length condemned to death by the Senate he committed suicide to avoid execution.

53. *Dives:* See the parable of Lazarus and the rich man in St Matthew's Gospel, ch. 16. The word is now used as a proper name, and applied (usually in a disapproving sense) to any wealthy person; but 'dives' is merely the Latin for 'rich man', not the name of a particular rich man.

Joint stock: joint-stock companies working with capital provided jointly by a number of partners or shareholders.

Trust, or Combine, or Kartel: groups of manufacturers or financiers who agree to certain measures—limitation of output, uniformity of prices, exclusive selling areas, etc.—in order to control or prevent competition.

54. *workhouse:* Under the Poor Laws which formerly operated in England but have been abolished, destitute and aged people without means to feed, clothe, and house themselves were provided for in public institutions called workhouses. The treatment was sometimes harsh, and the workhouses were generally disliked. Pensions and other forms of public assistance now allow needy people to live in their own homes.

Mr Rockefeller: John Davison Rockefeller (1839–1937), American millionaire who gave vast sums of money for educational, religious, health, and scientific purposes, through the Rockefeller Foundation and other agencies.

Sunday School: religious classes, mainly for children, meeting on Sunday mornings and afternoons. The Sunday Schools were started in England by Robert Raikes (1735–1811), a Gloucester newspaper owner, in 1780, and spread throughout Britain in the nineteenth century.

55. *dreadnoughts:* large armoured warships with heavy guns, so called after the British battleship *Dreadnought* (1906).

Job: the central figure in the Book of Job in the Old Testament.

potsherd: a broken fragment of pottery.

feed his lambs: See St John's Gospel, ch. 21, v. 15.

anomaly: used here in the sense of 'unevenness' or 'disproportion'.

nine-tenths of the wealth: since Shaw wrote this, heavy taxation of the rich in Britain, higher wages for the working classes, and various social welfare measures, have brought about a great change in the distribution of wealth.

56. *mooted:* suggested; spoken of.

London School of Economics: founded in 1895 and now a recognized college of the University of London; it specializes in the teaching of economics and political science.

Judas Iscariot: the disciple who betrayed Jesus.

the Gadarene swine: See St Mark's Gospel, ch. 5, vv. 1-16.

the widow who put her mite in the poor-box: a mite = one-eighth of a penny. See St Mark's Gospel, ch. 12, vv. 41-44.

Horatio Bottomley: (1860–1933), English journalist and financial speculator; he was in prison for fraud from 1922 to 1927, having in earlier years cunningly defended himself against similar charges.

Jack Johnson: (1876–1946), American boxer; heavyweight champion of the world, 1908–15.

Palestrina: Giovanni Pierluigi (1525–94), Italian composer, called Palestrina from his birthplace near Rome. He wrote music for church services and was Master of Music at the Vatican.

Offenbach: Jacques Offenbach (1819–80), French composer of operas, mostly light and amusing, though *Tales of Hoffmann,* the best known, is more serious.

Sir Thomas Lipton: (1850–1931), British merchant who made a fortune from his grocery and provision stores; he was also a yachting enthusiast and tried several times to win back an international cup held by the United States.

Paul Cinquevalli: an exceptionally skilled and popular conjurer who performed in the early twentieth century in music-hall variety shows.

Florence Nightingale: (1820–1910), English hospital nurse who became famous when she took charge of the sick and wounded during the Crimean war (1853–6) between Britain (with France) and Russia. She entirely transformed the army medical services both during and after the war, often against bitter opposition and obstruction by officials.

Mrs Siddons: Sarah Siddons (1755–1831), the most famous of English actresses; her birth name was Sarah Kemble.

the common hangman: the official appointed to carry out the sentence of the Court on condemned criminals.

Barney Barnato: (1852–97), rose from poverty to become a millionaire from the diamond mines of Kimberley, South Africa, having been born in the east-end of London; he committed suicide by jumping from the ship on which he was voyaging from South Africa.

56. '*Use every man after his deserts . . .*': the exact words of the quotation (from Shakespear's *Hamlet*, II. i) are: ' Use every man after his desert, and who should 'scape whipping?'

Dr Crippen: an English doctor of medicine hanged on a charge of murdering his troublesome wife in the early part of the twentieth century; he was the first criminal to be arrested through the use of wireless telegraphy, a message being sent by that means to the ship in mid-ocean while he was attempting to escape with a girl companion (disguised as a boy) to the United States.

bookmaker: a man who lives by taking bets on horse and dog races, etc.

58. *parasitic . . . parasitism:* a parasite is a person, or animal, or plant that lives by drawing nourishment from another; the word is also applied to human beings who prey on others instead of working themselves.

59. *abortionist:* a person who deliberately kills an unborn child; or, as used here, one who prevents another's natural development.

60. *oligarchy:* government of the many by a few.

quacks: persons who offer remedies or put forward schemes which have no genuine value; pretenders.

61. *haggling:* disputing in a trivial or mean way.

Buffon: George Louis Leclerc, Count de Buffon (1707–88), French naturalist; author of a *Natural History* in many volumes (1749 onward) and other important books.

Butler: Samuel Butler (see note to p. 21 above).

Bergson: Henri Bergson (1859–1941), French philosopher. Shaw was much influenced by his writings, drawing the term 'Life Force' from Bergson's phrase *élan vital.*

Weismann: August Weismann (1834–1914), German biologist and author of important books on heredity.

Lord Rothschild: Lionel, 2nd Baron Rothschild (1868–1937); he founded a valuable private Zoological Museum on his estate at Tring, in the English county of Hertfordshire.

62. *midwife:* one who assists women at childbirth; now extended to any person or plan helping to bring about a desired end.

alembics: apparatus used in chemical laboratories.

NOTES ON THE PREFACE

62. *Morris's News from Nowhere:* a romance published in 1891 by William Morris, 'Nowhere' being an imaginary ideal country (somewhat resembling England in earlier times) where the application of socialist principles has given happiness and peace to the community.

62-3. *the deaf man will not object . . . ear trumpets:* British legislation passed since Shaw wrote this sentence does now provide ear trumpets (hearing aids for deaf people) at the taxpayers' expense under the National Health Service; and some orchestras (which include flutes) are now supported from public funds.

63. *Manchester:* one of the largest manufacturing towns in England.

Swift: Jonathan Swift (1667–1745), English satirist; *Gulliver's Travels* (1726) is his most famous work.

One of . . . Chesterton's stories: the story referred to is 'The Tremendous Adventures of Major Brown' by Gilbert Keith Chesterton (1874–1936) in his volume called *The Club of Queer Trades* (1905).

the ermine: English judges' robes are trimmed with ermine fur.

Determinism: a philosophical doctrine which asserts that a person's conduct and destiny are determined (controlled and settled) by factors (heredity, etc.) beyond his own personal powers of decision.

64. *Free Will:* the opposite of Determinism; those who believe in the doctrine of Free Will maintain that men and women are personally responsible for the conduct and direction of their own lives, inasmuch as they are at liberty to choose between good and evil.

fluxions: a theory of mathematics published by Sir Isaac Newton (see note to p. 44 above).

65. *drays:* heavy horse-drawn carts used for transporting barrels of beer.

malingerers: persons who try to avoid a duty by pretending to be ill or otherwise handicapped.

Predestination: the doctrine that everything that happens to mankind has been ordained by God; fatalism.

Shakespear's Isabella: the heroine in Shakespear's play *Measure for Measure.*

66. *Talleyrand:* Charles Maurice Talleyrand de Périgord (1754–1838), French statesman who served under the Revolutionary

government and later served Napoleon, being given by him the title of Prince. Talleyrand was a leading figure in European affairs until his retirement in 1834. Though a man of genius in diplomacy, his moral standards were low, and he worked for personal advantage as much as for his country's benefit.

67. *Wagner:* Richard Wagner (1813–83), German composer; he brought about a revolution in the writing of operas, by making the words and drama as important as the music. Bernard Shaw admired him extremely and wrote a study of his works, *The Perfect Wagnerite* (1898).

Millet: Jean François Millet (1814–75), French painter; best known for his paintings of peasants in the fields.

nun: a Christian woman who enters a religious house or convent and so separates herself from the world.

68. *henpecked:* dominated by a masterful or scolding wife (as a hen may peck and worry a cock fowl).

69. *concupiscence:* lust; immoderate sexual desire.

Getting Married: the title of one of Shaw's plays (1908).

70. *scapegoat:* originally a goat set loose in the wilderness after a Jewish priest had laid upon it, symbolically, the people's sins; now applied to anyone who is blamed for the faults of others.

their feet should be beautiful on the mountains: a reference to a passage in the Book of the Prophet Isaiah (ch. 52, v. 7)—'How beautiful upon the mountains are the feet of him that bringeth good tidings, that publisheth peace.'

marital duty: the duty owed to each other by husbands and wives.

apron strings: persons are said to be tied to a woman's apron strings when (either as mother or wife) she limits their personal freedom and controls their lives: also applied to persons who cling too closely to a mother or a wife.

71. *vagabonds:* aimless persons with no settled purpose in life; tramps or wanderers.

Ibsen: Henrik Ibsen (1828–1906), Norwegian playwright and poet, who attacked conventional European standards of conduct. His works include *Brand* and *Peer Gynt*.

72. *lama:* a Buddhist monk in Tibet.

fakirs: wandering and begging holy men.

N

72. *Deans and Chapters:* the principal ecclesiastical officer (Dean) and governing council (Chapter) in the administrative affairs of a cathedral.

Joan of Arc: (?1412–31), French national heroine who led the army against the English and freed her country. See Bernard Shaw's play *Saint Joan* (1923).

Clare: St Clare, who founded a convent at Assisi in Italy about A.D. 1212 to practise the teachings of St Francis; like him they chose poverty, and are called 'the poor Clares'.

Teresa: Teresa de Avila (1515–82), Spanish nun and religious mystic, and one of the foremost saints of the Roman Catholic Church. Thérèse Lisieux (1873–97), a French nun, is also called St Teresa.

rake: a person who leads a disorderly or immoral life.

73. *the vanguard:* those who go in front or act as leaders.

Home Rule: government of a country by its own people. At the time Shaw wrote this Preface, 'Home Rule for Ireland' (since achieved) was an important political issue.

Insurance Act: National health and unemployment insurance began in Britain in 1910, introduced by David Lloyd George. It was at first bitterly opposed by well-to-do people, but is now regarded as the foundation of the Welfare State.

74. *The Way of All Flesh:* a novel by Samuel Butler (see note to p. 21 above) published shortly after his death. It is largely an account of his own early life with a father whose religion he found tyrannical.

sentient: living.

a wretched man and his wife: Ananias and Sapphira (see the Acts of the Apostles, ch. 5, vv. 1-10).

harangue: a loud and dogmatic speech.

exordium: the introductory section of a speech.

75. *pathological symptom:* a sign of disease or abnormal mind.

76. *Robert Owen:* (1771–1858), English social reformer; wrote *A New View of Society* (1813).

Karl Marx: (1818–83), German-Jewish journalist and advocate of revolutionary Communism. Author of *Das Kapital* (1867).

ratiocinable postulate: logical assumption.

77. *Frankenstein's monster:* Frankenstein is the central character in a novel by Mary Shelley (1797–1851), wife of the English poet;

Frankenstein, or the Modern Prometheus (1818) tells of the construction of an artificial creature resembling a man; he becomes a hateful monster and in the end murders Frankenstein who made him.

77. *Atlases:* Atlas is the name given to the son of one of the Titans (giants) in ancient Greek mythology. The legend concerning him says that for taking part in the Titans' revolt against the gods he was condemned to carry the heavens on his shoulders. In modern pictures and statues he is shown supporting the earth as a globe, and his name is given to any book of maps (atlas).

Pragmatism: a system of philosophy which judges beliefs, moral ideas, etc., by asking 'does it work?' *i.e.* is it of practical benefit to men and women by increasing happiness and promoting good?

put your back into: a colloquial phrase meaning 'try with all your strength'.

Hedonism: a philosophy based upon the conviction that pleasure is the chief good in human life.

Stoicism: the philosophy originated by a Greek teacher, Zeno (third century B.C.); it was named after the Stoa (porch) in Athens where he and his followers met for discussion. 'Stoicism' is popularly regarded as a synonym for 'patient endurance', but the philosophy is more complex than that. One of its main principles is that no person and no thing is good unless it 'fulfils its function', *i.e.* does thoroughly well what he (or it) was created to do.

No-ism: a word invented here by Shaw to suggest the negative habit of believing in nothing, or having no faith in anything.

78. *Carlyle and Ruskin:* Thomas Carlyle (1795–1881), Scottish historian and essayist; John Ruskin (1819–1900), English art critic, essayist, and writer on social reform. Further study of their lives since Shaw wrote suggests that some modification is needed in his statement that they 'defied the tyranny of sex'; it now appears, rather, that their shrinking from sex was due to psychological complications in their lives.

79. *patent medicine:* any remedy for which extravagant claims are made. The term goes back to the time when manufacturers of such remedies could apply for an official licence (called a

'patent') which prohibited competitors from imitating the product.

80. *malversate:* corrupt.

81. *Calvin:* See note to p. 13 above, on Luther and Calvin. His doctrines had a deep and lasting influence in Scotland and Switzerland.

fatalisms: beliefs that regard every event and every personal experience as inevitable and unavoidable because it is predestined by Fate.

the famous ode to charity: i.e. ch. 13 of the First Epistle of St Paul to the Corinthians (in the New Testament).

83. *Geneva:* the city in Switzerland which was at one time the stronghold of Calvin's doctrines.

Knox: John Knox (?1505–72), Scottish Protestant religious reformer, much influenced by Calvin.

nosing out: searching for in a malicious or interfering way.

Holy Willies or Stigginses: names given contemptuously to self-righteous and hypocritical persons; from 'Holy Willie's Prayer', a poem by Robert Burns (1759–96), and Mr Stiggins, a character in *Pickwick Papers* by Charles Dickens (1812–70).

Puritans: the seventeenth-century religious enthusiasts who broke away from the established Church of England and took the Bible as their sole guide. The word 'puritan' is now generally applied to anyone who holds extreme religious views or is rigid in moral conduct.

84. *to 'get up':* to study laboriously and mechanically, without enthusiasm or genuine personal interest; to study merely for the purpose of passing an examination.

Molière: Jean Baptiste Poquelin (1622–73), who called himself Molière; the most famous French writer of stage comedies.

Hugh Latimer: (1485–1555), English bishop; he was burned as a heretic in the reign of Mary I, the Roman Catholic queen, for refusing to renounce Protestantism.

monger: purveyor; dealer; trader.

Mosaic: according to the law of Moses as given in the Old Testament. (Not to be confused with 'mosaic', a picture or other design made by embedding small cubes of glass or stone in cement.)

85. *did not matter a rap:* was not of the slightest importance.

PAGE

85. *eating the god:* the consuming of bread and wine in Christian Church services signifies the sacrifice of the body and blood of Christ.

parthenogenetic birth: virgin birth; without sexual union between human parents.

the Trinity: Father, Son, and Holy Ghost, the threefold nature of godhead in orthodox Christian belief.

Arian: Arius (*c.* A.D. 256–336) founded a movement which taught that Jesus was created by God before all the rest of Creation and that he was therefore wholly divine, not the God-man as the New Testament teaches. Arianism was attacked by the Christian Church as a heresy.

Nestorian: the Nestorians are an eastern Christian sect, holding doctrines considered heretical by other Christians.

excommunicated: the Roman Catholic Church from time to time passes a sentence of excommunication upon heretics and other serious offenders against its doctrines; those thus sentenced are excluded from communion with members of the Church and are cut off from all spiritual contact with them.

Charlemagne: i.e. Charles the Great, or Charles I (A.D. 742–814), Emperor of the West from the year 800.

86. *Albi:* in the eleventh–fourteenth centuries a sect originating from Albi, in Provence, France, preached against what they considered to be the corrupt state of the Roman Catholic Church and were branded as heretics by the Pope. They were called Albigenses, and their righteous and austere mode of living brought them many followers in spite of persecution.

the Inquisition: a Roman Catholic organization set up in A.D. 1248 to seek out heretics and bring them to trial and judgment. It operated in several countries, most notoriously in Spain, and was governed from Rome by a special body named The Congregation of the Holy Office, which continued (with the purpose of controlling printed publications) after the Inquisition, as such, came to an end in Spain in 1834.

massacre of St Bartholomew's: The Huguenots (French Protestant Christians) throughout France were ordered by King Charles IX and his mother Catherine de Medici to be murdered in massacres timed to begin on St Bartholomew's Day (24 August) 1572.

Gustavus Adolphus: (1594–1632), Gustavus II, king of Sweden

N 2

from 1611, and a victorious general in campaigns against Russia, Poland, and Germany until he was killed in battle.

86. *Frederick the Great:* (1712–86), King Frederick II of Prussia, whose military skill made his country powerful; he also had intellectual interests and was for several years the patron of Voltaire (see note to p. 150 below).

Antichrist: an imagined superhuman opponent of Christ whom the early Christians expected to appear on earth before the world came to an end a thousand years after Christ, as they believed it would. Later believers have attached the name to certain powerful historical persons whose actions have violated the teachings of Christ.

Torquemada: Tomás de Torquemáda (1420–98), a Spanish monk who in 1483 became the Chief Inquisitor and was responsible for much cruel persecution and killing of condemned heretics.

Ignatius Loyola: (1491–1556), a Spanish soldier and man of pleasure before he took to the religious life and founded in 1534 the Society of Jesus, the members of which are called Jesuits. They take vows of purity, poverty, and obedience, and are bound to carry on propaganda for the Roman Catholic Church. They are still a powerful body and their influence is greatly exercised through schools in which a high standard of general education is combined with the skilful inculcation of religious doctrine.

Laud: William Laud (1573–1645), Archbishop of Canterbury; he imposed heavy punishment upon those convicted of holding beliefs contrary to the doctrines of the Church of England, but was charged with high treason while Oliver Cromwell ruled during the Commonwealth period, and was executed.

George Fox: 1624–91; founder of the Religious Society of Friends. Fox believed that God speaks direct to the individual soul without need of priests, and he opposed all church-going. The Friends are still an active and much respected Society; they oppose all war on conscientious grounds, but do a great deal of valuable and courageous work in war-time ambulance and hospital units and in other humanitarian work. They are commonly called Quakers, a name first used in derision by a judge whom Fox urged to 'tremble [or quake] at the Word of the Lord'.

86. *the vernacular:* a people's native language.

  Koheleth: the Hebrew name of a sage (wise man) whose beliefs are set forth in the Book of Ecclesiastes in the Old Testament. Ecclesiastes is the Greek form of Koheleth.

  the Pentateuch: the first five books of the Old Testament: Genesis, Exodus, Leviticus, Numbers, and Deuteronomy.

87. *psychopathy:* the study of mental disease.

  St Dunstan: (A.D. 924–88); Archbishop of Canterbury from A.D. 961. A legend tells that he was visited by the Devil disguised as a woman.

  Swedenborg: Emanuel Swedenborg (1688–1772), Swedish mystic; the Swedenborgian sect (or 'New Church') founded in London in 1778 is still active.

  Blake: William Blake (1757–1827), English poet, painter, and engraver; he was influenced by Swedenborg's teachings.

88. *Napoleon's Book of Fate, Old Moore's Almanack, and handbooks of therapeutic herbalism:* publications for simple and superstitious people which pretend to foretell the future, or describe remedies that can be made from common herbs.

  Huxley: Thomas Henry Huxley (1825–95), English writer on philosophical, religious, and scientific subjects. He described himself as an 'agnostic', *i.e.* one who is convinced that nothing can be known concerning the existence of God nor of anything that does not exist in material form. His best-known book is *Man's Place in Nature* (1863), and his writings in general provoked much contemporary disputation.

  Mahatma: a holy or great-souled man.

  Simon Magus: See the Acts of the Apostles (ch. 8, vv. 9-13), in the New Testament.

  Baptist: a member of the self-governing Christian Nonconformist body which holds that baptism by immersion is an essential ceremony.

  Congregationalist: a member of the Christian Nonconformist body which is controlled by appointed members of the congregation.

  Ingersoll: Robert Green Ingersoll (1833–99), American lecturer and author of books opposing Christianity.

  Bradlaugh: Charles Bradlaugh (1833–91), English social-reformer and rationalist. He was elected a Member of Parliament in 1880 but was not allowed to take his seat because he refused to sign the usual religious oath of loyalty which was then required of all members. He was repeatedly re-elected, however, and in 1886 was at length admitted to Parliament.

88. *Shelley:* Percy Bysshe Shelley (1792–1822), English poet; his unorthodox opinions on religion, morals, and politics led many of his contemporaries to treat him as an outcast.

Sir William Crookes: (1832–1919), English chemist and physicist; he discovered a new element (thallium), made valuable studies of radioactivity, and invented special lenses for eyeglasses.

Dunglas Home: Daniel Dunglas Home (1833–86), American spiritualist whom many people suspected of trickery, though nothing could be proved against him. 'Sludge, the Medium' by the English poet Robert Browning is an attack on Home, in whom Browning's wife Elizabeth Barrett Browning believed.

Karma: the Hindu and Buddhist doctrine that successive states of existence are higher or lower according to the person's (or creature's) goodness or badness in preceding stages of life.

metempsychosis: transmigration of souls.

89. *table-rapping Spiritualists:* at Spiritualist séances, messages from the dead are supposed to be received through a system of knocking-sounds on a table.

Gladstone: William Ewart Gladstone (1809–98), British statesman, leader of the Liberal Party, and one of the greatest Prime Ministers.

congenital: inborn; inherited.

90. *Higher Criticism:* study of the Bible by expert scholars who use scientific and critical methods of inquiry not approved by Christians who accept the Bible as the inspired and infallible Word of God.

91. *the Sermon on the Mount:* delivered by Jesus as described in St Matthew's Gospel, chs. 5-7, and in St Luke's, ch. 6, vv. 20-49.

jerry-building: hasty construction with materials of low quality.

synthesis: putting substances (or ideas) together to build up another substance or theory; the opposite of analysis.

Ussher: James Ussher (1581–1656), Archbishop of Armagh (in Ireland) from 1625. He put forward the theory that the date of the creation of the world was 4004 B.C., a date accepted by many Christians for centuries after Ussher's death but since entirely discredited by geological evidences.

91. *prepossessions:* prejudices; fixed ideas.

   protoplasm: the basic substance of animal and plant life.

   pontificates: speaks (like a pope, or pontiff) with a dogmatic air or with a conviction of infallibility.

92. *though his sins be as scarlet:* 'though your sins be as scarlet, they shall be as white as snow'—see the Book of the Prophet Isaiah, ch. 2, v. 18, in the Old Testament.

   napping: asleep; unaware.

   rank and file: originally 'common soldiers'; ordinary people; followers.

93. *Socrates:* See note to p. 30 above, on Plato.

94. *a whip of scorpions:* 'My father hath chastised you with whips, but I will chastise you with scorpions.'—The First Book of the Kings (ch. 12, v. 11) in the Old Testament.

   proselytizing: preaching with the intention of converting hearers to a particular faith or doctrine.

   Hume: David Hume (1711–76), Scottish historian and philosopher; his chief work was *A Treatise of Human Nature* (1739–1740).

   Joshua's campaigns: described in the Book of Joshua, in the Old Testament.

   Whately: (1787–1863); English religious writer; he became Archbishop of Canterbury in 1831; his *Christian Evidences* (1837) was much approved and often quoted by Protestant believers when answering opponents.

   Edward the Confessor: (died 1066), king of England from 1042; his deeply religious life earned him the title 'Confessor'.

   St Louis: (1214–70); King Louis IX of France; while taking part in the 7th Crusade he was captured in 1250 and, though he was soon ransomed, remained in the Holy Land until 1254; he died of plague while on a later Crusade.

   Don Quixote: See note to p. 46 above, on Cervantes.

   Mr Pickwick: the central character in *Pickwick Papers* (1836–7), a novel by Charles Dickens (1812–70).

   Macaulay: Thomas Babington Macaulay (afterwards Lord Macaulay), British historian, essayist, poet, and statesman; lived from 1800 to 1859; he spent five years in India, from 1834, as a member of the Supreme Council appointed by the British government.

94. *Grimm:* two German brothers, Jacob Ludwig Carl Grimm (1785–1863) and Wilhelm Carl (1786–1859) wrote famous books on the history and structure of language, but are better known by the stories they collected and published as *Grimm's Fairy Tales* (1812–15).

95. *Lao Tse:* Chinese philosopher (sixth century B.C.) and supposed founder of the religion known as Taoism.

96. *Bishop Colenso:* John William Colenso (1814–83), English religious writer and mathematician who became Bishop of Natal (South Africa) in 1853. His critical examination of parts of the Old Testament (*The Pentateuch and the Book of Joshua Critically Examined*, 1862–79) was bitterly attacked by the authorities of the Protestant Church (to which Colenso belonged) and he was removed from his bishopric, but when he appealed to the Privy Council his removal was declared to be illegal. He upheld the cause of the Zulus and protested against their treatment by the Boers (South African Dutch) and the British.

uncial . . . cursive: styles of writing used in early manuscripts; uncial resembles modern capital letters; cursive is a rapid, or running, style and closer to modern handwriting.

Pascal: Blaise Pascal (1623–62), French writer on religion who was also an accomplished mathematician and scientist. His *Pensées* ('Thoughts'), published after his death, are still widely read.

D'Aubigny: Jean Henri Merle d'Aubigné (1794–1872), French religious historian and Protestant preacher; wrote a *History of the Reformation* (1835–53).

St Jerome: (*c.* 340–420), Christian scholar whose translations of the Scriptures were used for the Roman Catholic (Latin) Bible called the Vulgate, the title of which is taken from a Latin word meaning 'to make public' or to bring into general use.

Genesis: the first book of the Old Testament.

Progressive: a Liberal in politics and believer in measures for human progress through social reform.

Collectivism: the political doctrine which aims to bring land and all means of production and distribution into national (*i.e.* collective) ownership.

State Churches: religions which are recognized and officially approved or supported by the secular authority.

96. *Byron's Cain: Cain* (1821) is one of the poetic tragedies written by the English poet Lord Byron (1788–1824). It deals with the story of Cain's murder of his brother Abel, told in the Book of Genesis, ch. 4.

Salvation Army: a Christian missionary organization started in London in 1878 by William Booth (1829–1912). It has since extended its work throughout the world, and its officers use titles of military origin, its head being known as General. General William Booth named the organization Salvation Army because he intended it to make war on all kinds of sin.

the tight little Island of Britain: the phrase 'right little, tight little island' was probably first applied to Britain in a popular patriotic song in the nineteenth century, in reference to the fact that the island is tightly protected by the sea which surrounds it.

97. *defender of the faith:* a title borne by British monarchs from the time of Henry VIII (reigned 1509–47); he denied the authority of the Roman Church but retained the title (*Fidei defensor*) given him previously by the Pope.

we islanders are only forty-five millions: all the statistics in this and the following paragraph relate to the year 1915 and are no longer accurate.

'disciples of Christ': Disciples of Christ is the title used by a Protestant Christian sect started in the United States of America in 1811 by Alexander Campbell. The members take the Bible as their sole guide. Since Shaw wrote this Preface, their membership has increased very considerably and they have established themselves in other countries. They are also called 'Campbellites' and 'Churches of Christ'.

Nonconformist: The English Nonconformist Churches are those which broke away from the Church of England in the seventeenth century. Early in the present century the Nonconformists opposed the government's Education Act, which gave grants of money to Church of England schools, and they refused to pay taxes which financed the schools. Their household goods were liable to be seized and sold to provide the tax money, and those Nonconformists who continued to refuse payment went to prison.

98. *parochial delusions:* mistaken views due to inability or refusal to take account of affairs happening outside a narrow area;

parochial = belonging to a parish, the smallest area in English local administration.

98. *Jehovah:* the English rendering of one of the Hebrew names for God in the Old Testament.

Krishna: one of the gods in Hindu religion.

Zoroaster: (or Zarathushtra) founder of a religion which flourished mainly in Persia; he lived in about the sixth century B.C.

'*Absent thee from felicity awhile*': a quotation from Hamlet's dying speech in the last scene of Shakespeare's *Hamlet*.

baffle: perplex; disconcert.

putting on hair shirts: a medieval form of self-punishment or penance, intended to benefit the soul by the infliction of pain or discomfort on the body; the phrase is now applied figuratively to any attitude of mind which produces extreme self-criticism, or to any belief involving self-denial.

99. *heterogeneous:* mixed.

Trappist: a Roman Catholic monastic Order, the members of which lead an extremely ascetic life and observe a rule of silence. They took their name from the monastery at La Trappe in France.

the thirty-nine articles: a set of rules and principles governing the clergy of the Church of England; they are printed in the English Prayer Book.

the Westminster Confession: a document drawn up in 1643 by the Assembly of Divines which met at Westminster to advise the English parliament on a settlement of the religious differences then troubling the nation. Though it was intended to replace the Thirty-Nine Articles, the Westminster Confession became the rule only of the Presbyterian Church of Scotland.

100. *Ulster is refusing to accept fellow-citizenship:* a part of Ulster is now self-governing, with the title Northern Ireland; the remainder of the country is now the Irish Republic (Eire). Northern Ireland chose to remain a part of the British Commonwealth, though it has its own parliament.

Bossuet: Jacques Benigne Bossuet (1627–1704), French theologian and preacher. He was a great orator and delivered famous funeral addresses on some of the leading people of his time; he also wrote important works in defence of Roman Catholic doctrine.

Belfast: the capital city of Northern Ireland.

100. *the Vatican:* the palace of the Pope in Rome and the international headquarters of the Roman Catholic Church.

Sir Henry Stanley: (1841–1904), English explorer and traveller in Africa, where he sought for and found in 1871 the famous Christian missionary David Livingstone, who had disappeared into the interior.

Baganda: the African people of Uganda.

Senegalese: the people of Senegal in (French) West Africa.

Petrine ... Pauline: according to St Peter ... according to St Paul.

prophylactic: preventive; safeguard.

101. *Jewish canonical literature:* the Old Testament and the Talmud which contain the religious law of the Jews.

The open mind: a state of mind without personal convictions and open to consider all points of view.

intestate: without leaving a will which gives instructions concerning the disposal of property.

moves only as the cat jumps: a colloquial phrase applied to a person who does not act independently, but waits to see what others will do.

brigand: one of a band of robbers.

the negative man: a man without positive convictions or principles.

Cromwell: Oliver Cromwell (1599–1658), English leader of the Parliament armies against King Charles I and his Royalist supporters in the Civil War (1642–6; 1648–51); appointed Lord Protector of the Commonwealth of England, Scotland, and Ireland in 1653. He was strongly Protestant in religion and therefor antagonistic to Roman Catholics.

cannibalism: the eating of human flesh by other human beings.

laid him by the heels: colloquial phrase meaning 'put him under restraint'.

disparaged: spoke against; belittled.

Long Pig: human flesh.

102. *St Sophia:* originally the Christian Church at Constantinople (Istanbul), afterwards a mosque, now a Turkish national museum of Byzantine art.

sacristan: the officer who acts as caretaker of a church or other sacred building.

the laity: laymen; ordinary members of a religious body, as distinct from priests or ministers; also applied to people in general who have no expert knowledge of a particular subject.

102. *anti-Clerical:* antagonistic to the control of religious communities by clerics (*i.e.* priests or clergy).

Kruger: Paul Kruger (1825–1904), President of the Transvaal and leader of the Boers against the British in the South African War (1899–1902).

the divine right of kings: for many centuries there was a widespread belief that kings derived their authority straight from God and were not subject to parliaments or other human control. The English king Charles I was executed in 1649 after being condemned on charges which denied his claim to rule by divine right.

Tweedledum . . . Tweedledee: twin characters in the children's story *Alice Through the Looking Glass* (1872) by Lewis Carroll, the pen-name taken by Charles Lutwidge Dodgson (1832–98), a famous mathematical scholar at Oxford University.

NOTES ON *ANDROCLES AND THE LION*

Prologue

103. *pampered:* treated with too much care and indulgence.

     slattern: an untidy, dirty, and lazy woman.

     the prime of life: the time when a person's health and strength are at their best.

104. *you glory in it:* you are proud of your behaviour.

     a laughing-stock: a person who is ridiculed or made fun of, either because he is weak and timid or because he behaves foolishly.

     a shrew: a scolding and bitter-tongued woman.

     butter wouldnt melt in your mouth: a colloquial phrase meaning that the person referred to is gentle in manner and voice.

105. *stout:* fat and bulky.

     dont take on: don't upset yourself; don't allow yourself to be distressed.

106. *Andy:* her familiar diminutive for Androcles.

     Meggy: familiar diminutive for Megaera.

107. *ums tootsums wootsums:* Androcles talks to the lion in the kind of baby language that English mothers use to soothe their infant children; in such language 'tootsy-wootsy' refers to a baby's foot.

     make velvet paws: sheathe your claws.

     Steadeee: steady.

Act I

109. *triumphal arches:* The ancient Romans built magnificent arches in their cities (chiefly in Rome) to celebrate the triumphs of victorious leaders of their armies.

     debouch: come together in an open space.

     campagna: countryside (Italian).

     centurion: a Roman officer in command of 100 men.

     dogged: determined.

     cohort: a troop of Roman soldiers.

     larks: tricks.

     Coliseum: a great amphitheatre in ancient Rome, used for gladiatorial contests; many Christians were killed there during the persecutions. A large part of the Coliseum still remains.

109. *gladiators:* men trained to fight with swords or other weapons at the public games in ancient Rome; they fought either against other gladiators or against wild beasts.

patrician: member of a noble family; aristocrat.

110. *blasphemy of singing Christian hymns:* to pagans (such as the ancient Romans) Christian hymns would seem as profane and offensive as the singing of pagan songs would seem to Christians.

Onward Christian Soldiers: a favourite Christian hymn which Shaw names here as typical of the kind of hymn that early Christians might have sung, though this particular one was not written until the nineteenth century, by the Rev. Sabine Baring-Gould (1834–1924).

forum: the meeting-place for speeches or public discussion in Roman cities.

111. *Tention!:* Attention!

Imperial Circus ... Imperial Menagerie: the Emperor's company of gladiators and wild beasts kept for combat in the chief Roman amphitheatre. During the persecution of the Christians, many who refused to deny their faith were thrown to the lions or set to fight the trained gladiators. Usually they refused to protect themselves and were mercilessly killed.

112. *sacrilege:* any offence against a sacred person or building or object.

a pinch of incense: as much incense (gum or spice burned in honour of a god and giving off a sweet-smelling smoke) as can be held between the forefinger and thumb.

clemency: mercy; mild treatment of an offender.

113. *titter:* giggle; faint laughter by a silly or a frightened person.

the tenth legion: the Roman army was divided into legions, each containing several thousands of men.

armorer: a maker of weapons and armour.

sorcerer: magician.

take his receipt, countersigned: get a written acknowledgment of delivery with additional signatures (by the officials named).

a nap: a brief sleep.

114. *humane:* kind; compassionate; showing tender human feeling.

flirting: pretending light-hearted affection.

voluptuaries: persons immoderately devoted to sensual pleasure.

rabble: noisy mob.

riff-raff: low-class people.

114. *Jupiter:* the chief of the gods in Roman mythology; called Zeus in Greek mythology.

Diana: in Roman mythology the virgin goddess of hunting; Christians refused to obey the Roman command to worship at her altar.

116. *trim:* smart.

retinue: a group of persons attending on or following someone of importance.

epicene: the term applied to a womanish man (as here), or to a mannish woman; a person having the characteristics of both sexes.

Lets chaff them: chaff = tease, or make fun of.

got a figure: has a well-shaped body; is physically attractive.

117. *starting:* making a sudden movement of surprise or alarm.

cad: an ill-mannered person, or one who offends against an accepted code of behaviour; sometimes applied by conceited people to those they consider to be on a lower social level.

Pull yourself together: control yourself.

What do you take me for?: a colloquial phrase, usually spoken indignantly when another person has assumed that the speaker will tolerate disrespectful or immoral behaviour.

plucky: courageous.

filly: literally, a young female horse; used colloquially by amorous men in reference to an attractive girl.

choleric: bad-tempered.

debauchee: an evil-living person; particularly one who leads others into depraved habits.

pals: a slang word for friends.

118. *sniffs:* a 'sniff' is the sound made by a tearful person when drawing air into the nose.

a Billy goat: colloquial term for a male goat (Nanny goat is the corresponding female term).

mobs: attacks as one of a mob or disorderly crowd.

one of the turn-the-other-cheek gentlemen: Christians are commanded not to resent or resist bad treatment, but to make their enemies ashamed by inviting further punishment. Jesus is reported to have said: '. . . resist not evil: but whosoever shall smite thee on thy right cheek, turn to him the other also. And if any man will sue thee at the law, and take away thy coat, let him have thy cloke also. And whosoever shall compel thee to go a mile, go with him twain' (St Matthew's Gospel, ch. 5, vv. 39-41).

119. *out of countenance:* embarrassed.

a shade of green flickers in his cheek: fear causes his face to turn so pale that his skin seems to have a greenish colour.

with paternal weight: with a kindly pressure such as a father might give to his son.

promptings: impulse; urging.

whacks: blows.

square: balance; equalize.

120. *Cappadocia:* a region of Asia Minor; now part of Turkey.

wrestling for his soul: striving to convert him to Christianity.

in the morning . . . his hair was as white as snow: There is a popular belief that severe mental strain or sudden shock will cause the hair to turn white in a few hours, though scientists say that no such rapid change is possible.

121. *with unction:* fervently.

backslidings: a backslider is one who falls away from the religion he had accepted and followed for a while.

providence: a supernatural guiding or protective influence.

122. *might . . . lay that gladiator out:* lay out = knock down; render unconscious; kill (slang).

123. *Ive drunk all my nerves away:* excessive indulgence in alcoholic drinking has a harmful effect upon the nervous system and may destroy the victim's ability to control his faculties.

the horrors: colloquial term for a drunken person's fits (*delirium tremens*), in which he imagines himself threatened by fantastic creatures or horrors.

124. *trot along spry:* move along quickly and smartly.

ox goad: a pointed stick used to make oxen or other animals move quickly.

125. *olives and anchovies:* one or other of these may be served at the beginning of a formal dinner to stimulate appetite.

emetic: a substance that causes vomiting; used now as an antidote to poison, but wealthy Romans are supposed to have used emetics at intervals during prolonged feasts in order to renew their appetite and enable them to continue eating.

Act II

126. *his eyes blazing:* so wild with anger that his eyes look as though they are alight.

   trident: a weapon with three prongs.

   a barred visor: the hinged and slotted part of a protective helmet, which could be raised or lowered.

   The editor of the gladiators: their manager; this is an uncommon use of the word, for an editor is more generally the man who is responsible for the contents (other than advertisements) of a newspaper or other periodical publication, or of a book.

   if the people turn down their thumbs: At the Roman contests the audience turned their thumbs downward if they wished the defeated gladiator to be killed by his opponent; if they wished him to be spared they turned their thumbs upward.

   talents: A talent was a unit of money or weight among the ancients; its value varied between, roughly, £200 and £400 sterling, according to the country and the period.

127. *vestal virgins:* women dedicated to the Roman goddess Vesta (the deity of the hearth); they were sworn to chastity and it was their duty to keep the sacred fire constantly burning in the temple dedicated to Vesta.

128. *Dog of an apostate:* a term of abuse meaning 'traitor'.

   Get thee behind him, Satan: when Peter attempted to persuade Jesus that his crucifixion was not inevitable, Jesus replied, 'Get thee behind me, Satan', meaning that he thought the Devil was at that moment using Peter as a mouthpiece of temptation.

   For two pins: a colloquial term meaning that very little persuasion would be required to induce the speaker to undertake the act mentioned.

129. *pugnaciously:* in a threatening manner.

   rotter: an abusive slang word for a person whom the speaker dislikes or despises, or considers to have behaved improperly or 'rottenly'.

   Devil a better!: a little-used colloquial term meaning 'none is better'.

130. *He bolted him before you could say Balbus:* he swallowed him very quickly. The equivalent modern English colloquial phrase is '. . . before you could say Jack Robinson'.

130. *bitters:* a liquor, usually drunk when mixed with gin; it is regarded as an appetizer (*i.e.* as stimulating appetite for food).

   bluff: without deference; a manner which suggests 'I am as good as you are'.

131. *touching his forelock:* a salute made by raising a hand to the hair of the forehead.

   your Worship: the English form of address to a magistrate.

132. *the Pretorian Guard:* the specially chosen soldiers who served as the personal bodyguard of Roman emperors.

   archangels: the chief angels (Gabriel and Michael are the best known).

   a dirty trick: an unfair action.

   sesterces: a *sesterce* was a Roman coin worth about 2d.

134. *in the sweet by-and-by:* colloquial phrase for 'in the happy future'.

136. *That passage is your hill to Calvary:* Jesus was crucified on the hill called Calvary.

137. *sardonically:* cynically and bitterly.

   bolted: ran away hurriedly.

   cur: a mongrel dog; the word is applied in contempt to a person who is considered worthless or cowardly.

139. *a hideous Etruscan mask:* The Etruscans were the ancient (pre-Roman) people of Etruria, a region in central Italy. Their art is now much admired, even though much of their sculpture is terrifyingly impressive rather than beautiful by modern standards.

140. *Domitian:* (A.D. 51–96), emperor of Rome from A.D. 81; his reign was a time of tyranny and bloodshed.

   a Gaul: a native of the country which is now France.

142. *the lot:* the fate.

   portcullis: heavy iron-barred gate which slides up and down in grooves.

   frisking: jumping playfully.

143. *high treason:* offences against the State or its ruler.

144. *bad wicked Tommy:* a playful term of affection with no plain meaning.

   coquettishly: as though he were a playful and flirtatious girl.

145. *bigoted:* immovably prejudiced.

146. *magnanimous:* generous in mind and spirit.

   opportunist: a person who behaves according to any advantage to himself that the opportunity of the moment offers, and not according to personal conviction or moral principle.

146. *Have-and-Holders:* Shaw's phrase for those in positions of power or wealth who are determined to hold on to what they have.

147. *Home Secretary:* the British minister for internal affairs.

Taste: 'Taste' in this sense is the ability to recognize and value what is beautiful and good. Shaw uses the word ironically here, as though it meant only obedience to current local standards of behaviour.

Free Churches: the British Protestant Nonconformist Churches, which are 'free' from official association with the Church of England.

148. *St Augustine:* (died in A.D. 604), Christian bishop and author of a famous theological work *The City of God* and of an autobiography called *Confessions of St Augustine.*

wrong uns: (wrong ones), bad people (slang).

The Devil's Disciple: one of Bernard Shaw's *Three Plays for Puritans,* written in 1897.

clergy: ministers of the Church of England.

Anthony Anderson: a character in Shaw's *The Devil's Disciple.*

They have turned their churches into recruiting stations and their vestries into munition workshops: Shaw is referring here, figuratively, to the support given to the British war efforts in 1914–18 by the clergy.

stuck to their livings: held on to their salaried positions in the churches.

When the Archbishop of York . . . .: a few prominent men in Britain during the 1914–18 war adopted a pacifist or conciliatory attitude which offended the majority of their countrymen.

149. *Freethinkers:* Shaw uses the word here not as the usual synonym for Rationalists, but as a term for those who think for themselves, not as authority or custom directs.

150. *Voltaire:* J. F. M. Arouet de Voltaire (1694–1778), French philosopher, poet, and playwright; he believed in the existence of God but attacked orthodox Christianity.

Peculiar People: a Christian religious sect founded in England in 1838; they take their name from references in the Old and New Testaments (Deuteronomy, ch. 14, v. 2; 1 Peter, ch. 2, v. 9; Titus, ch. 2, v. 14).

151. *the black flag:* when English criminals were hanged for murder a black flag was hoisted over the prison in which the execution took place.

the Albert Hall: a large building at Kensington, in west London, where entertainments and meetings of various kinds are held; it is mainly used for concerts of classical music.

Earl's Court: a district in western London, between Kensington and Hammersmith: it has a large building used for important industrial exhibitions and an arena for entertainments.

Anti-Vivisectionists: those who oppose surgical experiments on live animals.

Flat-Earth men: eccentric people who continue to believe that the earth is flat, not round.

the Crown Prince: eldest son of Wilhelm II, German emperor at the time of the first World War, 1914–18.